The Moon, the Hare, and the Pearl

An Intuitive Guide to the
Therapist-Client Relationship

*A Companion for Therapists and Others
Who Are Drawn to Their Inner Life*

JENAII GOLD, PH.D., MFT

CRONE PRESS

The Moon, the Hare, and the Pearl: An Intuitive Guide to the Therapist-Client Relationship — A companion for therapists and others who are drawn to their inner life, by Jenaii Gold, Ph.D., MFT. Copyright © 2020 by Jenaii Gold. All rights reserved.

This book may not be reproduced in whole or in part, in any form or by any means, electronic or mechanical, including recording, or by any information storage and retrieval system now known or hereafter invented, without written permission of the publisher. Brief excerpts may be quoted, in print or online, for the purpose of book reviews. For permission requests, contact the publisher below.

Crone Press
www.jenaiigold.com

Disclaimer: In the process of writing this book, I have drawn on case material encountered over the course of my professional life. However, all illustrations of case material are compilations from many sources and no one person has been used as an example of any idea. I value privacy very highly and have made every effort to obscure specific reference to any client.

Book Developer & Editor: Naomi Rose
www.naomirose.net

Proofreader: Gabriel Steinfeld
www.naomirose.net/proofreading-by-gabriel-steinfeld

Cover Illustration & Interior Illustration: Brenda Duke Murphy
www.bdmillustration.com

Book Design & Typesetting: Margaret Copeland, Terragrafix
www.terragrafix.com

The Moon, the Hare, and the Pearl: An Intuitive Guide to the Therapist-Client Relationship — A companion for therapists and others who are drawn to their inner life / Jenaii Gold

First edition. Published 2020.
Printed in the United States of America.

ISBN #: 978-1-7342365-0-7

"Cleverness is mere opinion, bewilderment is intuition."
— Jalal-uddin Rumi

"The things of this world are vessels, entrances for stories: When we touch them or tumble into them, we fall into their labyrinthine resonances. The world is no longer divided, then, into those inconvenient categories of subject and object, and the world becomes religiously apprehended."
— Lynda Sexson

Intuition (*L. intueri*, "to look at or into")

"I regard intuition as a basic psychological function (q.v.). It is the *function* that mediates perceptions in an unconscious way.... The peculiarity of intuition is that it is neither sense perception, nor feeling, nor intellectual inference, although it may also appear in these forms. In intuition, a content presents itself whole and complete, without our being able to explain or discover how this content came into existence. Intuition is a kind of instinctive apprehension, no matter of what contents.... The certainty of intuition rests equally on a definite state of psychic 'alertness' of whose origin the subject is unconscious."
— C. G. Jung

Dedication

I dedicate this book to my ancestors, to all those who have thought deeply and struggled to convey meaning for themselves and others. Their efforts have enriched my life. I dedicate this work to my parents, Evelyn and Daniel Goldstein; to my children, Adam and Lara Gold; and to their children, Camilo, Pele, and Mika, as well as to children to come. May these words be of service.

Acknowledgments

In Buddhist practice there is a prayer before eating that asks us to pause for a moment and acknowledge the many hands that have brought us this food and express our gratitude to them. We can give thanks to the plants and to the hands that planted them. We can acknowledge the person who picked them, prepared them, and perhaps even shipped them to us from a great distance. This backward turning and recognition offers us a way to experience our interconnectedness and interdependence with all of the things and people in our lives.

Similarly, in writing *The Moon, the Hare, and the Pearl*, I have felt the presence of voices from the ancestors, my childhood, my parents and their parents, and the echoes of writers whom I have never met but who have given me the gift of their work. All of these offerings have been integral to my ability and capacity to create this work. I sincerely hope that this book will serve others in a similar way.

Innumerable people have helped to forge my awareness and my skills. First, I want to express gratitude to my clients who allowed me to share their lives and who placed their trust in me. The relationship between therapist and client is as tender as a new green shoot breaking through the earth; it is subject to the weather, the nutrients in the ground, and the attention of the gardener who tends it. Both therapist and client plant the seed of a therapeutic relationship. Together, through their mutual effort, they discover what will come forth.

For over thirty years I have been very fortunate to work both as a therapist in private practice and as a supervisor in several agencies. These were nourishing places to work, and I am grateful for all that I learned there and for all that I was able to contribute. I want to thank my co-workers at Tulare Youth Services, The Phoenix of Santa Barbara, and the Family Service Agency of Santa Rosa. These agencies work diligently to contribute to the community and to those in need of care.

In my role as a supervisor, I met an extraordinary group of interns, all working hard on their way to licensure. The supervisor-intern relationship is complex and layered, involving a deep exchange of information within the frame of the supervisor's power to assess the student's progress. The relationship asks for honesty, vulnerability, and authenticity on both parts. Supervision has been a rich part of my work and I am grateful for the opportunity to have mentored so many wonderful students. We have laughed a lot and learned together. In that spirit, I offer my tricks of the trade to all who might find them useful in their investigation into the nature of who they are as a therapist and human being.

The creation of this book and of myself as a therapist has many roots, and in that context I wish to first express gratitude to my parents, who gave me a deep love and respect for learning, inquiry, and the beauty of the written word. My mother gave me the gift of her fierce intellect that asked questions and sought to know the truth. My father gave me the joy of his laughter and his love of music and people.

Early in my development, it was clear that ideas had great importance for me. In this way, Hermann Hesse — author, philosopher, and seer — filled a much-needed space in my psyche. Without his precious words, I would have felt alone in this world, lost among ideas with which I did not resonate, and all the while sensing that something beautiful and connected existed somewhere. *Journey to the East* and *Magister*

Acknowledgments

Ludi[1] were my touchstones. Yes, I realized, everything is interconnected. There is a path. There is a way.

In my late twenties, I met devotees of Guru Maharaj Ji, a young Guru from India. For many months I listened and learned about meditation and peace within. Maharaj Ji taught me how to go inside, meditate, and trust what I find there. I offer my deepest gratitude to him for showing me the perfect knowledge and the wisdom of turning inward.

Early in my career as a therapist I met Debra Manchester, Director of the Family Therapy Institute of Santa Barbara. Through her excellent training in family systems, I learned to think systemically and to step back and observe the dynamics and movement of energy within the family constellation. Her work encouraged me to be fearless and direct in my process, while remaining empathetic and sensitive to all who were present.

Much gratitude to the residents of The Phoenix of Santa Barbara. They taught me so much about the human heart, empathy, and the meaning of compassion. They showed me that the value of a human is far more important than any limited concept of truth or reality.

I was very fortunate to be able to continue my education at Pacifica Graduate Institute in Santa Barbara, CA, where I received my doctorate in Clinical Psychology with an emphasis in depth psychology. Gratitude to C. G. Jung, James Hillman, Robert Romanyshn, Marion Woodman, and the faculty of Pacifica Graduate Institute, who shared a language with me capable of expressing the beauty and depth of psyche-centered psychotherapy. When I entered Pacifica as a doctoral student, I knew that I had found a home. Pacifica is a sanctuary for the study and expression of soul, a rare gift in this world.

I cannot even begin to express my sincere gratitude to the marvelous and courageous women who laid down breadcrumbs for me to follow. I have carried their books around with me for many years until they have become worn and ragged with love and attention. I am grateful to Olive Schreiner; May Sarton; Clarissa Pinkola Estes, Ph.D.; Dora Kalff, Jungian analyst; Marion Woodman, Jungian analyst; Jean Shinoda Bolen, M.D. and Jungian analyst; and so many other extraordinary women who shared their wisdom. Olive Schreiner wrote *"We make a track to the water's edge"* — all of us, each of us, one by one bravely creating destiny.

I also want to acknowledge Sigrid McPherson, a Jungian analyst and my mother-in-law. Unfortunately, I knew her for only a few years before her death. I received four books from her that shaped my thinking as a therapist: *Memories, Dreams, and Reflections,* by C. G. Jung; *Alchemy,* by Marie-Louise Von Franz; *Jung and the Tarot,* by Sallie Nichols; and *The Lady of the Hare: A Study in the Healing Power of Dreams,* by John Laird, M.D. These books illuminated my path. I have reached for them at every hour of the day and night and I have found them to be an inexhaustible treasure. Each of these books inspired me to explore the work of C. G. Jung more deeply. His work has become the bedrock of my own understanding and articulation of psychotherapy.

I wish to offer deep gratitude to my Zen teachers Joko Dave Haselwood, Darlene Cohen, Jisho Warner, and many others who helped light my way. The path of Zen practice is always unfolding before me.

A special thanks to my dear friends Jean Meyer, Marianne Rothschild, Carol Gray, and R. A. McGregor, who have been my champions and who encouraged me to bring forth my words. A very special thanks to my editor, Naomi Rose,

Acknowledgments

who has worked with me since the inception of this book to the finish. She has truly been a midwife to my ideas and my process as well as keeping me afloat with affirmations of confidence and worth. Much gratitude to you, Naomi. We have traveled a long way together and I am grateful for our work and our friendship.

Good in the beginning, good in the middle, and good in the end. Much gratitude to my fabulous husband, who has listened and listened and listened! I could never have completed this daunting task without his kindness and patience. With great generosity, he brought his discernment, clarity, and wisdom to this endeavor. He has been a staunch protector of my lyricism, for which I am very grateful. He brought me unquestioning support and kindness at every turn.

Contents

Acknowledgments... vii
Preface.. 1
    Inception and Purpose.................................. 5
  Introduction: *Beginning the Journey* 11
Part I — Invoking Your Intuition 15
    Chain of Pearls: *How Everything Connects* 17
        Handmaidens of Intuition 21
        An Exercise in Intuitive Recall..................... 24
    Synchronicity: *The Coincidence of Time and Space*........... 27
    Filings to the Magnet: *Drawing on Your Inner Knowledge*.... 29
    Intuition: *The Self and the Four Functions* 35
    Following the Breadcrumbs: *The Tale of Hansel and Gretel*.... 41
Part II — Tricks of the Trade 45
    Backward Turning..................................... 47
    The Art of Attention 51
    Discerning Pattern 57
    Symptom as Messenger................................. 65
    Creativity and Addiction............................... 71
    Sitting with Loss...................................... 77
    Curiouser and Curiouser............................... 85
    The Gift of Sand and Water 89
    Playing All 88 Keys................................... 95
Part III — Psychotherapist as Trickster — or, Crazy Like
a March Hare 97
    The Sacrifice of the Hare and the Healing Dream 99
    Holding the Seat..................................... 107
    LOL 111
    Meeting the Gypsy 115
    Skillful Means.. 119

Part IV — On the Practice of Suffering and Joy........ 127
    Theater and Therapy 129
    Psychotherapy as Confession........................ 135
    Kindness Toward the Self 141
    In the Beginning Is the Ending 147
    Resist Contrivance 153
    Last Thoughts 159

Endnotes 161
About the Author 167

Preface

> *"Bringing forth what is within you requires the act of utterance. It is to communicate to another human being who you are: it is putting yourself in jeopardy, baring your jugular vein....*
>
> *To open yourself for the sake of another person is life-giving, as it was in the beginning when you first emerged from the womb."*
>
> —June Singer, *Seeing Through the Visible World: Jung, Gnosis and Chaos*[2]

While sitting in a coffee shop reading June Singer's book, *Seeing Through the Visible World*, I came to this passage. I felt as though I had been seen in a most intimate and challenging way. *Utterance*, I repeated the word aloud. To speak and to speak out; why did the act of giving voice to oneself feel so perilous? My interior life had always remained quite private. Although I had taught and worked in a deeply personal way, writing a book on psychotherapy seemed to require nothing less than baring my soul. The anxiety attendant to this literary process surfaces at times, much as it did when I began to paint at age 50; inner gates opened, and what had been hidden became visible and manifest. I write with gratitude for this opportunity to bridge my all-too-personal propensities with the greater good.

The Moon, the Hare, and the Pearl is a departure from most books on psychotherapy in that it takes an unusual tack. It does not promote a particular theory, nor does it demur from giving advice. Instead, it suggests a way in which the personal life of the therapist, including her struggles and challenges, becomes grist for the mill of her own awakening as well as contributing to a parallel process in her client. The intersection of lives in the therapeutic container creates a transformative, alchemical mixture for both client and therapist. Over the years, psychotherapy has been a practice of contemplation, deep questioning, and reflection.

For those readers interested in their inner life, *The Moon, the Hare, and the Pearl* offers insight into the intuitive relationship between client and therapist in depth psychotherapy. It suggests paths of exploration both within the therapeutic container and on one's own. It offers the gifts of metaphor and symbol as ways to move deeper into the understanding of the Self on the path to individuation.

Sometimes I am sitting with a client and they ask, "How do you listen to other people's troubles all day?" In actuality, this is a many-layered question and a worthy one. I usually say, "I do it because I see and hear something else, not only the troubles but something beautiful in the people who describe them. The troubles are like clouds moving across the night sky. Over time, the client and I become observers as we wonder about the winds, the weather, and what they portend." Like Ulysses, we set sail with great hope. The therapist has her maps and charts and she is adept at reading the stars. Nonetheless, the journey is perilous and full of surprises; and she knows that in the end, wherever that is, both she and the client will be changed through the experience. And so she sits and listens for openings and closings, for ways in and ways through the darkness and suffering.

Preface

Many years ago, when writing my dissertation, I began with this passage from the ancient Sumerian myth *Inanna: Queen of Heaven and Earth*.[3]

> From the Great Above she opened her ear to the Great Below
>
> From the Great Above the goddess opened her ear to the Great Below
>
> From the Great Above Inanna opened her ear to the Great Below.

This passage calls to me again as I begin writing this book. Wolkstein explains that in the Sumerian language, the words for *ear* and *wisdom* are the same; thus, bending one's ear to the Great Below becomes a transformative, alchemical act. Deeply listening is the stock-in-trade of the psychotherapist. Words resound through her ears and her body while impressions enter through her thinking, feeling, and intuitive faculties. The client's story mixes with her own personal and professional history, resulting in a synthesis of comprehension. At the same time she listens *to* the story that is being told, and *for* the story that is implied, unconscious and unspoken, as though a silent chorus is waiting to sing. This image serves me well in my work; the silent chorus waits in us all.

Similar to a Greek chorus, it is a vessel of reflection, warning, and revelation. Much of the time our interior lives are stifled in their expression, obscured by outer events and demands that distract us from pursuing a deeper connection to life. Meanwhile, deep within is a counter-veiling energy that yearns for expression through our dreams, art, and intuition.

Inanna: Queen of Heaven and Earth[4] is a deeply feminine myth that elucidates the flow of energy in the female psyche and also serves as a template for the journey of awakening in psychotherapy. The story follows the young and passionate goddess through a descent that takes her into the darkest regions of her soul. The story begins when Inanna *opens her ear to the Great Below*. She hears a call from the depths that she cannot ignore. Her sister Eriskegal, Queen of the Underworld, has summoned her to attend the funeral of her husband, Gugalanna, the Bull of Heaven. The sisters have been estranged. Metaphorically, heaven and earth, light and darkness, have also been separated. Inanna's choice to attend the funeral potentiates a change that is both planetary and personal. Her descent initiates a spiritual transformation through a journey of death and rebirth.

As Inanna begins her passage to the Underworld, she must descend through seven gates. At each one she surrenders an aspect of her persona, including her crown, her clothes, and her title — until she arrives stripped bare and bereft, both physically and psychologically. Eventually, when she meets her sister, Eriskegal kills her instantly and hangs her dead body on a meat hook!

Initially, I recoiled from the gruesomeness of this image. What could it mean? However, we must remember that we are now in a symbolic realm of Gods and Goddesses. Inanna has endured a descent, a process of psychological dismemberment, in which she has left all that was familiar to her to traverse new and unfamiliar territory. As the Goddess of Light, she is destined to meet her other half, her sister, the Goddess of Darkness. This is her path to completion.

Like the young goddess, most of us have experienced times when we felt as though all of the props and habits, circumstances and fortunes upon which we depended were no longer available to us. Our identity has been demolished, and we stand naked and unknowing. At these times, both men and women may hear the *call* and, without consciously intending it, set foot on a path of descent and return to a deeper and wiser relationship to themselves. The summons may come through the loss of a relationship or job, a spiritual epiphany, death, or illness — anything that has turned life upside down, leaving us feeling lost and unmoored. Taking the path of awareness often requires the sacrifice of old attitudes and patterns, which then allows space for new aspects of the personality to be included, integrated, and lived. During these difficult periods of challenge and transition, people may seek the help of a therapist to accompany them through their requisite descent and rebirth.

INCEPTION AND PURPOSE

The Moon, the Hare, and the Pearl initially grew out of my work as a supervisor of Marriage and Family interns and as a psychotherapist. It is in part a memoir as much as a work of counsel — a recollection of those times when I realized something true or valuable that stayed with me and shaped my thinking. I am writing from my perspective as a woman in her seventies who has worked as a psychotherapist for thirty-two years. The impetus to share these experiences comes in part from the archetype of the Crone or Elder, the wise woman who surfaces in the third stage of a woman's life. No longer young, she is not the innocent maiden nor is she the mother caring for the daily needs of her children. She is a Grandmother or great mother, and all that entails; overseeing the next generation and contributing a breadth of experience and the gift of reflection. Mothering now takes on a broader meaning: mentoring those around her and protecting the earth, our hearth and home. Her face is wrinkled, her eyes deep-set, and her countenance speaks to a profound engagement with life. She is called to the responsibility of adding her voice to the world's conversation.

The work of a supervisor embodies the energies of the Triple Goddess — the Maiden, the Mother, and the Crone. To be effective, she must remember what it feels like to be the Maiden, the ingénue, innocent and unsuspecting. As the Mother, she brings nurturance and guidance; and as the Crone, she embodies the steely wisdom of experience. For a male supervisor, there is a parallel development. He needs to nurture as a loving father who brings his support and guidance. He, too, is called to remember the state of innocence common to all young people, as he brings the wisdom of the Wise Old Man archetype forward to sustain and enrich those in his care. What a witch's brew!

In addition to helping guide *new therapists*, this book is intended to offer renewal and affirmation to *experienced therapists* — those who have been working in the field for some time and who may feel in need of inspiration or even a good laugh! Being a therapist is a lifelong journey of learning and challenge. An experienced therapist is like a polished stone in a river. Water has flowed over and around her for a long time, smoothing and shaping her edges and surfaces. She reflects the light that illuminates her. But like everyone, the therapist needs inspiration and companionship. She has times when her work feels full and alive, and other times when her energy wanes and she struggles against her own fatigue and aridity. Her work can feel solitary and demanding. May she find sustenance and enrichment through the compassion of the moon goddess, the trickster spirit of the hare, and the glowing wisdom of the pearl.

Preface

The symbolic trilogy of moon, hare, and pearl creates a foundation for exploring the way of intuition as a methodology in psychotherapy. Long ignored as a psychotherapeutic tool, intuition opens the therapist's perceptual field in a most unique way. When engaged with a client, we tend to rely on the immediacy of our thoughts, feelings, and senses. We may be less aware that intuition acts as a quiet but influential voice that guides us as we work. *Chain of Pearls*, *Filings to the Magnet*, and *Following the Breadcrumbs* are the intuitive *modus operandi* of the therapist, her tools of attunement to messages issuing from psyche.

Many therapists function intuitively to a large degree, although it is rarely spoken of or identified as such. In a world that proposes to be rational, our intuitive faculty is often overlooked or interpreted as irrational, irrelevant, and certainly unreliable. It is frequently designated by gender, as in "women's intuition" — as though it belongs *exclusively* to women. The assignment to women is most likely intended to devalue perceptions that cannot be readily validated. In general, this innate sensitivity meets skepticism in a world that prizes rational thinking as the most reliable form of understanding and comprehension, although some of the greatest discoveries — in science, for example — have been made intuitively. Artistic endeavors can also be highly intuitive, as well as spiritual experiences and pursuits. We understand that women work collaboratively from both hemispheres of the brain. This allows them to apprehend information in a more complete and complex way that creates a pathway through the literal to a metaphoric understanding. This capacity enhances our ability to work in a deeply complex way and facilitates connection to unconscious material.

In my writing over the years, I have honed a voice that does not pander to subject/object as the only viable means of expression. Perhaps you have noticed a little trick in the writing program on your computer that wants to change your writing from the so-called passive voice to the active, "masculine" voice. It much prefers this direct form of communication, no doubt finding it more efficient. I have done my best not to submit to this insistent editor but, instead, to stay closer to the heart of a metaphoric presence.

I must take a moment to explain that I live with two different vocabularies, each highly intuitive in its way. The first derives from C. G. Jung and Archetypal Psychology. Jung's mythopoetic basis is intrinsic to my depth-oriented work. The second, my practice and study of Zen Buddhism, has taught me that impermanence and emptiness reside at the core of all experience. Zen practice has deepened my understanding of compassion and non-judgment as a path in both my personal and professional life. These two languages commingle in a description of a figural world inhabited by Buddhas and Boddhisatvas, gypsies and tricksters, as well as Artemis, Aphrodite, and her many sisters who call out to me at 4 a.m. and say, "Get up and write this down right now!" These two rivers combine to provide a rich flow of impressions from which I draw inspiration and wisdom.

In the process of writing this book, I have drawn on case material encountered over the course of my professional life. However, all illustrations of case material are compilations from many sources and no one person has been used as an example of any idea. I value privacy very highly and have made every effort to obscure specific reference to any client.

I feel exceedingly fortunate to have chosen the work of psychotherapy. It is a privilege to sit with another person in

Preface

this intimate way. Over the years it has become a practice — not a formal meditation, but not so different, either. When I listen to a client's thoughts and concerns, I know that within them is a deep source of healing and renewal. We may call it Soul or Self, Buddha nature or God. Knowing this allows me to find joy and meaning in what I do. Now, in writing this book, I have the opportunity to give utterance to all that has been born and ripened within me in this practice. It is my sincere wish that reading *The Moon, the Hare, and the Pearl* will serve as an invitation to bring your idiosyncrasies, tenderness, curiosity, and power to the heart and soul of your practice.

— INTRODUCTION —

Beginning the Journey

The trick is to turn the eye inward, loosen the threads of our stories, and bring energy and curiosity to our inner life.

Most of us who have entered the profession of psychotherapy have been drawn to it by a desire to unravel the mystery of our own lives and actions. We have sought healing in different ways, and most likely continue to do so. At the same time, we know how to listen and empathize with the concerns of others. We are curious about what moves us as human beings, and we are intrigued by the mystery of what is beyond our understanding. We are attuned to the suffering of others, and we sense a capacity and desire to be a healing force. Having been a psychotherapist for over thirty years, I have had more than enough time to discover some tricks of the trade that I would like to pass along to my fellow tricksters. For that is who we are — magicians, actors, seekers, artists, and healers.

Not only am I writing about tricks of the trade but I have been tricked into writing. Several years ago, I awoke in the middle of the night with the idea of writing a primer on the practice of psychotherapy called *Tricks of the Trade*. It was not surprising that this creative idea would arise out of the darkness of dreamtime, where it had been incubating. Previously, in my waking state, I had confronted the idea of writing a book but I had dismissed it as overwhelming. On this particular night, however, a masculine dream voice spoke seductively. "It's okay, it can be a primer, short and sweet, no big deal!"

"A primer? Yes, I can do that," my ego replied. Psyche knew just how to present the idea so that I would bite.

It is now six years later, and my primer has morphed into a longer work: *The Moon, The Hare, and the Pearl*. Ironically, I find myself the object of my own trick, an unwitting recipient of my inner trickster. The trickster has been present throughout the whole of my process in the form of the *hare*, a wonderful, long-eared creature, swift of mind and instinct, which surfaces in the early hours of dawn as well as in the evening, when the sun begins its descent into the ocean. At these times, I find myself most receptive to impressions of all kinds. The book has taken on a life of its own, unwilling to conform to my constraints.

People often come to psychotherapy in search of something they cannot name. Perhaps they hope to find some part of themselves that they have lost or never really known. They may be struggling with anxiety and depression. Their lives have become untenable despite their best efforts to deal with their difficulties. The client hopes that the therapist possesses some magic or wisdom that can be conveyed to them, when in reality the therapist is there to guide them in discovering and securing his or her *own* wisdom. As therapists, we do not possess the peace that they seek; but that is one of those beautiful scarves that swirls about us in the dance that we will do together, for there is a bit of deception in the art and artifice of psychotherapy.

Artifice is defined in the dictionary as "a clever trick or stratagem, cunning, ingenuity and inventiveness."[5] We might say that artifice is the shadow of art. A painting, for example, is a representation of the artist's imagination and, as such, is an offering and an opening into the artist's vision. Painters who employ visual perspective do so in order to enhance their work, to represent it in the way they imagine it to be. We, as observers, accept the contrivance. As therapists, the way we suggest and intimate what is truly ineffable is the art of our delicate conversation, because we cannot address directly what is at the heart of the matter.

We know that the peace a client is seeking resides within herself, "under her own pillow," as my Guru used to say.[6] However, the therapist cannot simply tell her to look under her pillow, where she will find it. Instead, therapist and client need to undertake the journey together. The search begins when they form a working alliance to uncover what has been forgotten and obscured. The trick is to turn the eye inward and bring energy and curiosity to the inner life.

The importance of accompanying another person in search of something extraordinary became clear to me when I read *Mount Analogue* by Rene Daumal.[7] The book begins with the protagonist's discussion of his desire to climb a mountain, an inner mountain, that connects heaven and earth. He writes:

> I could not regard this as a simple allegory, this idea of an invisible humanity within a visible humanity. Experience has proven, I told myself, that a man can reach truth neither directly nor alone; an intermediary must exist — still human in certain respects yet surpassing humanity in others.... But the very fact that there are two of us changes everything. It does not become twice as easy, no; from being impossible it becomes possible.[8]

Many times in life we struggle to resolve things on our own, believing that we need to be strong, independent, and self-sufficient. Daumal reminds us *that a man can reach truth neither directly nor alone.*[9] Thus, the union between therapist and client begins when they agree to climb the mountain *together* because that is what it will take — nothing more, and nothing less.

— PART ONE —

Invoking Your Intuition

Chain of Pearls
How Everything Connects

Synchronicity
The Coincidence of Time and Space

Filings to the Magnet
Drawing on Your Inner Knowledge

Intuition
The Self and the Four Functions

Following the Breadcrumbs
The Tale of Hansel and Gretel

Chain of Pearls

How Everything Connects

In this time of forgetting and remembering, it is impossible to be certain when it all began; but that everything is connected like a chain of pearls, this I know.

When I was four years old, I watched my mother hunched over a drawing board late at night, engulfed in the smell of charcoal pencils and rubber cement. Even at that age I knew that she was absorbed in her work and that she was unavailable to me. Watching her creative torment left me fearful of my own artistic impulses. As I grew older she asked me into the studio to model clothes for her. As a fashion artist she was always in need of a hand or a head. She draped me in clothes much too big for me and I would stand as still as I could until restlessness or rebellion won out.

Sensing my mother's inner struggles, I directed my energies toward school and more literary interests. Art seemed too dangerous, and it was fifty years before I began to paint. Now that I am in the midst of my own artistic angst, I feel her presence around me like a chain of pearls. I, too, sit in my studio early in the morning and like her, a cup of black tea is always close at hand. Her intensity and one-pointedness surround me like a familiar cloak.

Some years ago, I awoke from a dream in the middle of the night with a chain of pearls twisting like a double helix before my eyes. The image so captivated me that I wrote it on a piece of paper and taped it to the bottom left-hand corner of my computer, along with two additional descriptors of how I know what I know: "filings to the magnet" and "following the bread crumbs." The double helix appeared as two intertwined ropes of sparkling pearls twisting like a molecule of DNA.

Jane Markell, a Jungian analyst, suggests that "the labyrinth or maze, the spiral or wave-like patterns of consecutive spirals, or a double helix moving toward the center and out again all illustrate attempts to be freed from old patterns of consciousness or stereotypes of order."[10] At the time of the dream, I was unclear as to its particular meaning, but that it held a great importance for me was clear. I wondered, what stereotypes in me were changing and loosening? What was asking to be born? In what way was I being constrained by old patterns?

Shortly after awakening from the dream of the double helix, I went into the living room in search of my familiar green book *Alchemy*,[11] by Marie Louise von Franz. I wondered if there was an alchemical counterpart to this unique dream experience. Sorting through and under piles of books, I was unable to find it. Instead, I found an art book, brought over by my neighbor Glen earlier in the afternoon. He had been to the Gleaners and returned with a shopping bag full of assorted treasures: door knobs, drawer pulls, and a book of art titled *Soutine* by Andrew Forge.[12]

The moment Glen spoke Soutine's name, something electric stirred in me and I asked to borrow the book. I put it on a table in the laundry room and went to bed without opening it. Upon awakening, I retrieved the book — and recalled seeing a reference to Soutine the previous day at the Contemporary Jewish Museum in San Francisco. I had been reading about

Jewish artists, and his name had been mentioned alongside Chagall's. I was curious that I had never heard of him; and now, within a matter of a few hours, he appeared at my doorstep once again! The synchronicity of the moment was unmistakable.

On the book's cover is a striking portrait of a young man in a red hat and coat against a dark background. His face is contorted, his head an irregular shape, angular like a diamond. He presents on the page so intimately — not back at a distance, but very present, with deep, melancholy eyes. It is unusual in every way, commanding in its tone and intensity. As I read the introduction to the book, I learned that this painting belonged to a series of pageboys painted at Maxim's in Paris by Soutine. Again, I felt an unusual sensation, the result of inexplicable connections being made and pearls sliding onto a string. I had spent the previous evening making reservations for my husband's and my upcoming trip to Paris, all the while wondering what, in particular, we might do there since we had only a few days. We had planned to go to the Louvre and the Musée d'Orsay; but now I felt quite clear and purposeful. I would try to see Soutine's work.

As I continued reading, I learned that Soutine was born in Lithuania to orthodox Jewish parents who had no interest in artistic expression and, in fact, felt that it was sinful. Determined to follow his creative instincts, Soutine left Russia as a young man and went to Paris in 1913 to pursue his vision. Andrew Forge, Soutine's biographer, suggests that we look at Soutine's art in terms of his *inner necessity*.[13] I felt shaken by the precision of this phrase, as I have described my own creative experience in a similar way. Both painting and writing feel less like a choice and more like a call from the unconscious that must be heeded.

The facts of Soutine's life felt like scraps of information, wisps of identity, through which I was connecting to my own DNA. I was particularly curious about his Lithuanian heritage, as my own Eastern European roots were similar. Soutine's father, like my grandfather, was a tailor. Perhaps, I thought, the uncertainty I often experienced surrounding my identity had been hanging in the air like a question without my being aware of it. Now, through the archive of the collective unconscious, a connection was occurring. I had a sensation of moving backwards in time and an unmistakable feeling of synchronicity and events coalescing in a remarkable manner across time and space.

Forge writes: "His art is supremely personal. He seems to be painting as we look. His pictures seem to be saturated by his presence, to reek of him."[14] These evocative words took me into a deeply personal place, where pearls tumbled about me like balls in a bingo cage. Then one was singled out and slipped onto a string. How does ethnic experience shape art and how is it passed on? I wondered. How does the intensity of our struggle to survive as a people bring us intimately into relationship with all beings? It was now almost morning, first light, and I crawled back to bed.

Several months later, my husband and I went to Paris and visited the Musée d'Orsay. After waiting an hour or so in a light rain, we entered the museum. Instead of going up to additional floors, we descended the stairs, going down several levels. On each floor was a unique and amazing collection of art. After several hours, we arrived at the very last exhibit. When I walked through the doorway, I encountered walls of paintings by Soutine. I was stunned by their power and intensity, and by a sense of inevitability that pervaded me. I had not consciously known about the exhibit, and yet here I was surrounded by this extraordinary display of human emotion and creative skill. I felt overwhelmed by the power of his work and by the synchronicity that had pulled me to this place in this particular moment.

When events fall together in this way, it is a mystery that opens up ways of understanding life that are not centered in the ego or the small self. Instead, we become aware of deeper, unconscious rhythms that move us. Each precious life is lived at both a personal and collective level, while experience persists across time like a chain of pearls. Most often we recognize only that part of the strand that we are aware of consciously; meanwhile, we are part of a much deeper, collective thread of humanity.

HANDMAIDENS OF INTUITION

Chain of Pearls, *Filings to the Magnet*, and *Following the Breadcrumbs* are my handmaidens of intuition. When I visualize this trio of modalities, I imagine the Greek statue of the *Three Graces*,[15] three women entwined, dancing together, moving in a synchronous way. This feminine image emerges from the nature of the intuitive process, itself, which feels inchoate, elegant, immediate, related, and connected.

What has this to do with doing therapy? *Chain of pearls* is a metaphoric way of describing how a therapist connects dots of meaning and deciphers patterns when listening to a client's story. To begin, I listen as I would to a dream, taking note of the landscape and the emotional tone. I notice the characters and their actions, while listening for psychological intersections that feel either charged or flat where there may have been traumatic experiences. I notice puns and metaphors as well as patterns of speech that suggest an intuitive sense of connectivity.

For example, some time ago a young woman, Darlene, came to the office. She was in her late thirties and dressed casually. I noticed that her face was pale and tense. I asked what had brought her in. She described her concern about a recent illness from which she had not recovered. She explained that although her physical symptoms had abated, she still felt anxious and oddly sad. Listless and unmotivated, she found herself procrastinating about returning to work. She described the progress of her illness, which began with the flu but developed into bronchitis. A course of antibiotics had been helpful, but her malaise seemed deeper. She felt sad and despairing.

Questions began forming in my mind. Why *this* illness? Why *now*? My mind associated to a particular reference in a book on *Traditional Acupuncture: The Law of the Five Elements*, by Diane Connelly, that I refer to in regard to illness. Connelly explains that: "The Chinese associated the deep and prolonged feeling of sorrow with the functioning of the lungs."[16] Over the years I have found this association to be true. When a person is sad, their hand often moves instinctively to the chest, over the heart and lungs. This is especially true when they are not breathing fully and are unable to take a deep breath. Connelly's use of the word "sorrow" seemed particularly apt in Darlene's case. I intuited a kind of throbbing in her presence, like a drum beating slowly under her words. Sitting with Darlene, I found myself drawn to her past. I was curious about other periods of illness in her life. I wanted to know about her parents and her relationship to them; something in her voice felt terribly young and vulnerable.

I asked her if she remembered other times when this sadness had overtaken her. She immediately recalled a time when her mother had been quite ill after an accident at work. She had hurt her back quite severely, and after the fall had stayed immobilized on the living room couch for months. Darlene was ten at the time. Her mother was unable to attend to her or even communicate more than a few words. She was often sleeping or on pain medication. Her mother never fully recovered from the accident, and their relationship was deeply changed. The enforced separation from her mother clearly still haunted her. Now in her thirties, unmarried and unattached, Darlene felt like she was still that little girl waiting for a kind word and attention, some recognition and caring from the mother she felt she had lost.

As she spoke, she had a far-off look in her eyes. While watching her, I imagined a chain of pearls, connecting her childhood feelings to her present situation. Her own immobility had triggered fear and distress while simultaneously evoking childhood memories. "She was never the same," she gasped sadly as she referred to her mother. Then the tears came. Her sadness had been buried for a long time. Re-experiencing her grief and anger around this period of separation from her mother was the starting point for seeing into her own emotionally-charged illness. As she continued in therapy Darlene recognized a pattern of avoidance in her personal relationships, opportunities when she had withdrawn out of fear of loss and pain. She was able to understand and hold with compassion the pain of her childhood without being hobbled by it. She was a courageous woman who became enlivened and emboldened to take steps to create a new future for herself. I appreciated her willingness to allow me to accompany her through this tender passage.

As I listen to a client, I give myself permission to associate to their story, to move away from a literal description into a more metaphoric presence by asking myself what this story evokes in me. How am I moved? These open questions allow me to access my intuition more easily. In Darlene's case, I sensed her anguish and loss, perhaps even a broken heart. I allowed myself to go into my own feeling of heaviness and bodily sensation. Feeling her deep sadness and loneliness, I breathed more slowly, taking it in. I allowed my body to speak to me.

Diane Connelly writes: "When man is serene and healthy, the pulse of the heart flows and connects, just as pearls are joined together or like a string of red jade — then one can speak of a healthy heart."[17] I so appreciate her metaphoric description that links the physical and psychic realms, thus creating a chain of pearls. The experience of continuity and interconnectedness is of critical importance for the psychotherapist whose work with unconscious material illuminates her path.

An Exercise in Intuitive Recall

As a new therapist, how do you handle the *impressions* that you experience when first sitting with a client? While you are filling out the paperwork, what drifts to the top of your awareness? What niggling impressions return to you? Perhaps you check in with your body and notice that you are tense. Your neck is tight, your shoulders a little high, and you are aware of a slight throbbing at your temples. You could brush all this off with a cup of coffee or ibuprofen; or you could notice that whatever has just occurred set you on edge in some way. Now is the time for your curiosity to surface, the inner detective who stood by watching the whole thing. Was it the client's tone of voice or the subject matter that stayed with you? What emotions were evoked in you as a result of your interaction?

Did she remind you of someone? Did anything in your conversation feel uncomfortable and, if so, what was it?

Interns are generally taught to make notes in a prescribed manner that may preclude recall of more subtle and powerful associations. Working within the usual constraints and parameters may force you into thinking mode too quickly. Alternatively, you might try putting down your pen and taking a long, slow breath. Sit with yourself and let the winds of intuition carry you. Allow your thoughts to flow freely, to wander, picking up bits and pieces of the session as they will. Perhaps a song or phrase will come to your mind, or even a story.

Take your time and allow the associative process do its work connecting all the impressions that you have. Do not try to make sense of them too soon; rather, let them hang like clothes on a clothesline, each pinned separately yet still connected. This will allow your thoughts to fall together like filings to a magnet. Then you can return to the task of the note, which will reflect your more complete understanding. In addition, you will often have a better idea of where you want to go in the next session.

Synchronicity

THE COINCIDENCE OF TIME AND SPACE

Chain of Pearls, Filings to the Magnet, and *Following the Breadcrumbs* are maps and charts that overlap and interweave. In all three descriptors, synchronicity plays an important part, because each approach is sensitive to how events connect and collide at a particular time and space. C. G. Jung, in his forward to Wilhelm's translation of the *I Ching*,[18] writes:

> *While the Western mind carefully sifts, weighs, selects, classifies, isolates, the Chinese picture of the moment encompasses everything down to the minutest nonsensical detail, because all of the ingredients make up the observed moment.[19]*

Both linear and non-linear approaches can be considered together, as the therapist listens to her client's story. She notices the coming together of experience in a connected and synchronistic manner. Often a client will say that "this happened and then that happened" as they link events in time and memory. She may, however, interpret these events in a somewhat different way that allows for synchronicity or even fate to play a part. Trauma and repetition are signposts that suggest deeper, underlying themes. I also allow any associations of my own to be present as well that may be related to personal experience or mythic themes.

The dictionary defines *synchronicity* as a simultaneous occurrence of events that appear significantly related but have no discernible causal connection.[20] Jung coined the word in the 1950s and wrote an entire volume on its meaning.[21] Because we do not have a simple explanation for how the unconscious affects events in the material world, we also do not have a simple explanation for the experience of synchronicity. Sallie Nichols, in *Jung and Tarot*,[22] explains that "all images tend to materialize in this way: it is their nature to seek expression in outer reality. We often use the word "coincidence" to describe events that appear to arise together or coincide because our waking consciousness is generally linear and causal. The artist Michelangelo described images as 'visions that yearn to be born, to free themselves from the unconscious.'"[23] We are most aware of these visions through dreams, our nightly encounter with unconscious images.

The power of image to reveal and clarify is evocative. I use the sand tray quite frequently in my work with clients because it facilitates the liberation of images, as Michelangelo suggested. I am always intrigued by what image is called forth in this moment. When a client works in the sand tray, the result is a mixture of what she or he is aware of consciously; at the same time, whatever is preconscious or out of awareness has the opportunity to make itself visible.

As a therapist if you are open to experiencing how time and space come together in what often feels like magical coincidence, you will be more likely to notice synchronous events when they occur in your own life as well as in sessions with your client. As a result, you will have a reverence for the interconnectedness of time and space not determined by ego consciousness or will.

Filings to the Magnet

DRAWING ON YOUR INNER KNOWLEDGE

Intuition is always operating and available, but the trick is to tone down the volume of other ways of knowing in order to hear it. Making time and space for reflection allows the filings of intuition to come to the magnet of awareness.

"Filings to the magnet" is a way of intuitively experiencing how apparently unrelated events pull or fall together. The experience has a sensate quality, almost like a wind blowing in. For example, when a client session is over, I often ask myself, "What did I see, feel, experience? How was I moved or changed by what I heard and felt?" By asking these questions, I open myself to sensing the *pull of events* and intuiting how they adhere.

Not long ago I left a session with Louise, a middle-aged woman with short, dark hair who had an air of innocence and sweetness about her. She had an easy smile and engaging eyes, yet she complained of anxiety, helplessness, and depression as she recounted recent events in her life. She had been in more than one emotionally abusive relationship, and her description of her part in them was complex and ambivalent. I asked why she had come for treatment just now. She replied that, currently, she was unencumbered by a relationship and found herself questioning her circumstances.

When I reflected on the session, I recalled her hands and the way she had held them contained in her lap while describing her difficulties. Her contained posture felt at odds with something young and ardent that I sensed/intuited in her nature. Her persona was polite and controlled. As she spoke she minimized the pain in her relationships, tossing it off as no big deal with the hint of a smile. Although she felt passive and vulnerable, I sensed her strong desire to find herself.

As I continued in my reverie, a mythic story about a young girl who had lost the use of her hands came to mind. Perhaps the way she held her hands in her lap or her rather unnatural stillness, juxtaposed with a sense of anticipation, triggered my association. She had described her inability to protect herself, to take action when needed. I wondered what her hands might do if they were empowered. I wondered what tasks lay ahead of her. How could she connect to her intuition? How might paying attention to her dreams assist her? As these questions surfaced, I imagined filings being drawn to a magnet of awareness within her, that is, something that would illuminate a cause or pattern in her behavior of which she had been previously unaware.

The Story of the Handless Maiden, as told by Gertrude Mueller Nelson,[24] is a powerful story that begins with the betrayal of a young girl by her father. Seduced by the promise of wealth and success, her father, a miller, traded her hands to the Devil. This horrific trade was initially made unconsciously, as he agreed to give the Devil whatever was behind the mill as the Devil had requested. The father thought that he had promised the devil an apple tree, but, alas, this was not the case! When the miller's wife heard what he had done, she reminded him that their daughter was behind the mill and that this was what the Devil wanted. What a terrible bargain the father had made!

When the Devil came to collect his due, the daughter washed herself and drew a chalk circle around her. The Devil could not get near her. Furious, he said he would return the next day for the girl and she was not to do this again. This time the lovely daughter cried and cried so that her hands were quite clean and purified. Once again the Devil could not take her. This time he said he wanted her hands or he would take the miller instead! The daughter agreed to sacrifice her hands to save her father, and he allowed her to do so. The Devil came for a third time, and this time the daughter had cried so long that the stumps where her hands had been washed clean with her tears so that he had to relent. He could not take her with him.

The daughter was then faced with a choice. She could remain with her father, who would take care of her (although he had not done a good job so far); or she could leave home and go in search of her own strength, power, and capacity. She bravely chose to make her own way in the world. When she set foot on her own path to completion, she encountered many challenges, of course; but through each one she found her strength, fortitude, and most importantly, her handedness. She was not helpless — quite the contrary. She had many internal resources born of love and determination.

As my work with Louise continued, it was clear that her formality was superficial. Soon a delightful smile broke through as she described her youth. As a child, she had inclined toward poetry and art but had received no validation for these gifts from her parents — particularly her father, who had encouraged more practical pursuits. Eager for acceptance, she had abandoned her instincts and pursued endeavors endorsed by her parents.

Earlier in the session, I noticed that she was turned slightly in her chair, looking at the sand tray figures. I asked if she would like to use the tray. "Yes, indeed," she replied. She began slowly, initially just moving the sand, adding water, and creating subtle landscapes. As she molded the sand, she became more comfortable with the medium, often creating gentle spirals. Louise worked in the tray for several weeks before adding a figure of a small child standing alone. We did not talk about the meaning of her tray but rather about her experience in making it. Did she enjoy the process? How was it for her to work in the sand? "It was calming and peaceful," she said. We stood together, looking appreciatively at what she had created. By staying in silence, we kept the meaning of the tray safely encapsulated, allowing whatever needed to come to light to arrive in its own time without explanation, pressure, or intellectual interference.

In later sessions, Louise added more figures to her trays, creating what appeared to be a new landscape for her life. At the same time, I noticed that she had begun moving more freely in the room as she worked. She chose a basket to hold the miniatures. Soon she took more than she needed. She sorted and sifted carefully. Meanwhile, she became more forthcoming in her verbal process as she described her childhood and its consequences. She renewed contact with a younger part of herself who had taken an interest in writing. I watched as she became increasingly animated. Through her work in the sand tray, her imagination was ignited and her helplessness and depression began to recede.

Louise started a dream journal and began to bring her dreams to our sessions, some of which were nightmares that had haunted her for some time. As she began to pay attention to her dreams, she realized that she had her own source of wisdom within. Seeing Louise coming into a deeper connection to herself was like watching filings coming to her inner magnet. They had been there all along, suspended and dispersed, but now her work called them in. Her process appeared highly intuitive. She seemed to rely upon an inner guide, a kind of unfolding intelligence waiting to find expression once she felt safer and connected to herself. In this way, she experienced her wisdom coalescing around her inner magnet or soul.

Intuition

The Self and the Four Functions

The practice of psychotherapy is much enhanced when both therapist and client invite and open to intuitive knowing. Intuition is often a doorway into numinous or spiritual experience that becomes increasingly important in the healing process. A client begins to trust what she cannot see but nonetheless knows is true. It is a validation of and by the Self. Intuition is a way into our more introverted aspects, our inner-directedness that balances a more extroverted perception and experience of the world. When a person enters therapy on a journey of self-discovery, a force is calling, making its presence felt like an inner magnet. Jung called this force the *archetype of the Self*. James Hollis, a Jungian analyst, describes it in this way:

> *Together, we have been humbled by our joint encounters with the Self; Carl Jung's metaphor for that inherent, unique, knowing, directive intelligence that lies so wholly beyond our ordinary ego consciousness. The metaphor of the Self arises from our intuitive knowledge that something within each of us not only monitors our organic biochemical processes, develops us from less complex to more complex creatures, but, much more, seeks that state of being that is the apparent purpose of our incarnation in the first place.*[25]

Like Jung, Hollis is speaking to an intuitive element in psyche that connects us to our deepest core. It is primordial, archetypal, and beyond the personal self. Recently, my daughter-in-law asked if it was possible to teach intuition. What a great question, I thought. I do not know that it can be taught, but it can be encouraged. To allow our intuition to take its rightful place at the table, we need to lessen our dependence on other ways of knowing. If we depend too much on thinking or feeling, we are less likely to hear the quieter voice of intuition. Having feedback from the sensation function is pivotal for grounding. If a person is a highly sensate type, that is, if sensation is their dominant function, all other functions are subsidiary. Over-reliance on any one function puts us in peril of not having sufficient access to other points of view, both internally and externally.

In Western culture, our reliance on the thinking function is the status quo or default option. When we are faced with uncertainty, we are told to "think about it." We are not told to quiet our minds, be patient, and allow our intuition to guide us, although our "sixth sense" is always operating and available. If we want to access our intuition, the trick is to tone down the volume of other ways of knowing in order to listen to it.

Intuition is like the air we breathe; it comes so naturally that we often fail to acknowledge its presence. Recently, on the evening news, I heard a scientist speaking about finding a ninth planet whose existence he intuits and infers from its impact on other celestial bodies around it. No one has seen the new planet, and yet he is quite convinced that it exists. Listening to him reminded me of how the intuitive process operates. Intuition is non-linear. It leaps like a hare across a green field, making wonderful associations and connections, with no need to explain how it got there. It can be amazingly quick, taking in many factors at once, processing, distilling, collating, and coalescing into a conclusion or impression. Intuition is synergistic; meanwhile, its methodology remains inchoate.

Intuition

Many psychotherapists function intuitively to a large degree, although it is rarely spoken about or identified as such. How else can we make the instantaneous choices that we do in a complex conversation with a client? The *thinking* function alone is too slow. The *feeling* function guides us in valuation but is often one-sided. The *sensation* function provides bodily feedback, but it takes a *combination of these capacities* to allow a therapist to assess, evaluate, respond, connect, empathize, and express in any given moment. Balancing the four functions enhances the individuation process, Jung's description of becoming more whole and complete as an individual.

Jung described the intuitive function as "irrational."[26] He explained that his use of the word, however, did not denote "something contrary to reason" but rather "beyond reason, something, therefore, not grounded on reason."[27] He further explained that thinking and feeling are both directed functions that "are in complete harmony with the law of reason," while both sensation and intuition "are functions that find their fulfillment in the absolute perception of the flux of events."[28] This is an amazing description. So Zen!

You can find an in-depth discussion of psychological types in Volume 6 of the *Collected Works: Psychological Types*, by C. G. Jung,[29] where he explains that the four functions "together produce a kind of totality." An understanding of these functions helps the therapist identify ways in which a client perceives the world and operates in it. It may also suggest a pathway to a more balanced orientation.

When working with couples, for example, it is useful to notice differences in their communication styles that are influenced by how each member of the couple perceives and processes information. Thinking and feeling types, for example, can easily misunderstand one another and usually do.

Each finds the other person very frustrating. Realizing their differences in perception allows each person to ease their tendency to blame the other when, in reality, each is speaking in a different language. Through enhanced awareness, they can begin to work toward more balance in their communication styles and are better able to experience empathy and compassion for one another. I should add that humor is especially helpful — in fact, essential — when doing this kind of work with couples. You gotta laugh!

It is most valuable to have all four functions in conversation with each other, each lending information and insight according to its capacity. However, for most of us, our dominant function leads the way, often brushing aside other information or points of view. In my case, intuition has been my dominant function. I tend to be quick and certain in my perceptions and conclusions but also impatient with the process of others, particularly thinking types who take the time to figure things out rationally. My inner magician feels that, with one swoop of her magic wand, all will be revealed!

Here is another example. I began playing the piano at four years of age. Having a good ear for music, I could replicate many things I heard, which I found very enjoyable. However, when I was older, my piano teacher wanted me to practice scales. I would have none of it. Too boring! I never mastered the piano because, in this way, I refused to take the time to build a more pragmatic foundation. Instead, I relied on my depth of feeling and intuitive sense of the music to carry me through. Writing this book, however, has stretched all of my functions and enhanced their ability to play well together. I have had to be more patient and methodical, careful and detailed — so difficult and yet so necessary in order to convey my thoughts and feelings with clarity. This book has been a practice in patience, perseverance, and an increased dependence on my thinking and sensate functions.

Jung wrote that each function contributes essential components to our understanding of our world and our location in it, so that whatever effort we make to strengthen what is weak and temper what is overly strong is of value. Each function has its special gift; and when they are all working together, we humans function like a well-oiled machine — on all four cylinders!

As psychotherapists, we accompany our clients as they navigate the uncertainties and flux of their lives, just as we do our own. Allowing intuition to take its rightful place at the table allows each of us to become increasingly at ease with new experiences. Intuition opens us to a multiplicity of factors and forces without necessarily being able to explain or justify them. Our intuitive faculty asks us to trust that we are more than we know and that our lives are informed in mysterious ways.

Following the Breadcrumbs

The Tale of Hansel and Gretel

"Wait a little, Gretel, until the moon gets up, then we shall be able to see the way home by the crumbs of bread that I have scattered along the way."
— "Hansel and Gretel," *Grimm's Fairy Tales*[30]

Perhaps you recall the fairy tale *"Hansel and Gretel"* by the brothers Grimm.[31] The story takes place in a time of famine and depletion, as many fairy tales do. Although fairy tales, like myths, speak to important themes in our culture and ourselves, fairy tales address unconscious motives in the guise of a simple story. This fairy tale is one of innocence, abandonment, courage, and growth.

As an only child, I resonated with this story in many ways. I longed for the company of a sibling to buffer the difficulties of a family triad as well as the sheer pleasure of having a friend and companion. Many times I found myself alone in situations that were frightening, as all children do. I often walked alone to school, music lessons, and literally through the woods to grandmother's house. I learned to observe my surroundings with great care, always making a mental note of the landscape so that I could find my way home. I could not know then that these solitary walks provided a methodology for finding my way home that I would later call *following the breadcrumbs*. This skill became essential in my work as a therapist later in life. The story of two abandoned children begins in this way:

The Tale of Hansel and Gretel

A poor woodcutter and his wife lived on the edge of a forest with their two children, Hansel and Gretel. Although the woodcutter worked very hard, they were poor and often did not have enough to eat. After the children's mother died, their father remarried. Unfortunately, their stepmother was cruel and unfeeling. [As we soon find out, the lack of a loving mother often sets the stage for things to unravel in fairy tales, as in life.]

One day, the stepmother insisted that the woodcutter take the children into the forest and leave them there to fend for themselves. Reluctantly, their father complied with this dreadful demand.

[As a child, I always wondered why he felt so compelled to do this. Why didn't he take *her* into the woods?]

Meanwhile, Hansel heard them hatching this plan and he made a plan of his own. He gathered small, white pebbles that would shine in the moonlight, thus marking a path to return home. His plan actually worked; but soon after the children returned home, their stepmother insisted that they leave once again! This time, the children took breadcrumbs to mark their way; but they did not count on the birds that followed along behind, eating them up. As a result, Hansel and Gretel found themselves utterly alone and lost in the dark forest far from home.

The metaphor of the forest is common in fairy tales, and aptly applies to those times in life when we find ourselves lost in confusion, away from our usual touchstones and resources. When we are in the forest of darkness, we may find enchanted beasts or other creatures and helpers as well as challenges that take us toward our ultimate goal, although they are most often in disguise. The forest is a place of mystery, where our ordinary daylight vision does not serve us. Thus, it is important to note that the children find their way by the light of the mother moon, a feminine presence, rather than the solar masculine. Some things are better found in darkness.

> After some time, Hansel and Gretel came upon a clearing in the woods, where they discovered a gingerbread cottage. Imagine their surprise and delight. They began to nibble happily at the roof; and just as they had begun to have their fill, a voice asked, "Who is nibbling at my cottage?" The children answered, "It is the wind," and continued to eat, ignoring the reality that the house was not theirs to consume. Soon an old woman appeared and invited them into the cottage. She fed them and put them to bed. The children felt safe and happy. Their apparent good fortune, however, was short lived, because the cottage belonged to the wicked witch. Who knew? She had taken them in, planning to fatten them up and eventually eat them. This would have been their fate, had Gretel not been a very clever girl. One day, as the witch was testing the oven for their demise, Gretel pushed her in and slammed the door shut!

[I always appreciated that it was *Gretel* who outsmarted the witch, and not her brother!]

> With the witch gone, the children explored the cottage and, to their delight, found gold and jewels. In their captivity, they had also found their own jewels of courage and ingenuity. Now their thoughts turned toward home; and in the marvelous and mysterious way that fairy tales unfold, a benevolent swan appeared to fly them home. [The swan is often considered a spiritual symbol that glides over the waters of emotional trouble with serenity.] Upon their return to the little cottage, the children learned that the

wicked stepmother had died, and once again they were reunited with their father. Their family was now whole, and they lived happily ever after.

"Following the breadcrumbs" is a metaphoric way of describing how to follow the path of your clients as they speak and unfold their tale. As you listen, take note of those places that have a resonance, a subtle and soulful calling. Follow the psychological breadcrumbs that link to one another like a serpentine path in the moonlight. My assumption is that clients are in search of meaning and a deeper understanding of themselves. If you work with a sand tray in your office, you will notice how often clients use shiny stones and pebbles to connect one place to another like breadcrumbs. They are creating pathways and connections to places of imagination and sanctuary.

Sometimes, when a client is using the sand tray, they will place Dorothy and friends from *The Wizard of Oz*[32] on a path of stones. It is clear to me that they have begun their psychological journey toward transformation and individuation. Friends and allies are frequently present, as well as inner adversaries. The popularity of these figures speaks to the universality of the experience of journey, the power of the ruby slippers, and the heart's desire to return home to its spiritual source.

There *is* a home, a path, and a way. All of us are dropping breadcrumbs, albeit unconsciously, as we go along in life. Sometimes, the intuitive therapist as well as the client can catch the breadcrumbs of meaning before the birds eat them up!

— PART TWO —

Tricks Of The Trade

Backward Turning

The Art of Attention

Discerning Pattern

Symptom as Messenger

Creativity and Addiction

Allow Your Curiosity to Lead You

Sitting with Loss

The Gift of Sand and Water

Playing All 88 Keys

Backward Turning

> *We psychotherapists are researchers, sleuths, and lovers of mystery who take a careful history while watching and listening for the breadcrumbs that lead homeward. Historical recovery is an archeological dig that provides context for the therapist, as well as an opportunity for the client to describe and discover what has been hidden and forgotten.*

As a client tells her story, the therapist looks down a long tunnel into the past. This backward turning gives us a feeling for the tone of the client's life from the beginning, as if it were a musical composition. Some lives feel somber and lonely, like a cello playing in the dark. Some have been chaotic and dramatic, and sound like cymbals clashing, full of shock and trauma. We can sense the anxiety and tension of lives that were like drum rolls that did not end, where the children were incidental and always waiting for the other shoe to drop. We can sense feelings of aloneness and isolation where children felt unheard or irrelevant.

I cannot emphasize enough the importance of this process of historical recovery. Do not give it short shrift. It is an archeological dig that provides context for the therapist as well as an opportunity for the client to describe and discover what has been hidden and forgotten. When we fail to adequately address the early experiences of the child, we miss the felt sense and description of their formative landscape. We know that time has intervened and that recollections may not be literal, but that does not devalue the process—quite the contrary. The client's feelings and impressions that have carried forward help us to understand significant aspects of her current challenges. Telling the story creates an opportunity for the client to give voice to what has been previously unspeakable and unspoken.

We owe a debt to Freud. Yes, it often *is* the mother — well, not only, but we need to have a sense of what it was like for the client to be a child in her family. Who else lived in her home — siblings, grandparents, or possibly strangers? Where did he/she spend her time? Did she feel safe? Where did she hide? How did she play? What was the scent of the house? What does she remember? This kind of evocative inquiry allows recall of subtle feelings that can be obscured by merely a simple chronological recounting of events. Sometimes a client says that she cannot remember anything about a period of time. This suggests that memories are buried underground for good reason. Tread lightly at this point; but do not forget to return.

Taking a history carefully and thoughtfully communicates several things to the client. First, that we are interested in them and their story. We want to know where they came from, what happened there, and what brought them to us, here, *in this moment*. We ask, "Why now?" We listen with attunement, because that is our art, and our deepest and most soulful gift. Through attending, we come to understand how the client views herself in the context of her life.

We begin to discern a client's stance — how she sees herself in relation to her world. Is she the doer, the victim, or the bystander? Does she experience herself as central, or overly central? Do you, as the therapist, have the sense that she is aware of you and how you are taking her in, or is she self-absorbed? Does she seem present or distracted? The more conscientiously you take a thorough history, the more you will discern important patterns in the life of your client, as well as common themes that apply to how all of our lives unfold. At the same time, the particular attention you bring to the client's story sets the groundwork for a trusting, working relationship.

On the other hand (for there is always another hand), you may find yourself sitting with a client who repeats old stories and wounds and for whom the recounting seems only to solidify their point of view. Often, strong emotions and a sense of drama are the glue that holds the scenario together. This kind of repetition suggests that the events were traumatic and as a result, the client felt it impossible to move on. Like Hansel and Gretel the client has gotten lost in the woods, going round and round. Unable to find the breadcrumbs, she feels that there is no way back.

At these times, I find that working with a sand tray is especially helpful in shifting focus away from the familiar and repetitive story to an open field that invites unconscious images to arise. The medium of sand and water offers the client a new avenue of expression. In particular, the silent work of the tray serves as a counterpoint to more conventional dialogue. For the therapist, witnessing her client's process in the sand is another form of deep attention.

Taking a history sounds fairly straightforward, but how you *receive* the story is the trick. How you gather breadcrumbs that are being dropped along the way is where skill pays off. As I listen, my mind shuttles between past and present — what I know of why the client has come, and how the past illuminates the present. In addition, my curiosity and attention to detail convey an empathic response and a willingness to see the client as a unique individual with specific qualities and sensibilities.

I would like to diverge for a moment and take you along this line of thought to a paragraph I read just this morning in Jane Hirschfield's book, *Nine Gates: Entering the Mind of Poetry*. She writes:[33]

> Next comes the concentration of narrative, in which the event itself is the sinew that moves a poem forward. Storytelling, like rhetoric, pulls us in through the cognitive mind as much as through the emotions. It answers both our curiosity and our longing for shapely forms: our profound desire to know what happens, and our persistent hope that what happens will somehow make sense. Narrative instructs us in both these hungers and their satisfaction, teaching us to perceive and to relish the arc of moments and the arc of lives.[34]

Don't you love that phrase, "the arc of moments and the arc of lives"? As you listen to your clients, watch for how the arc is made and how the story unfolds itself. Parts and pieces begin to adhere, to cling and cluster around potent themes like a chain of pearls. Through the telling comes the possibility for meaning and connection. As Hirschfield suggests, it responds to our *"persistent hope that what happens will somehow make sense."*[35] For the client, the act of retelling her life's story "not only knits together the scattered fragments of a hitherto unexamined life, but also is a work of Eros."[36] Recovery is a work of love. Bringing compassion to our life's story is a transformative act.

The Art of Attention

Honor your subjectivity, your capacity to be impressed or pressed upon. Your vulnerability and sensitivity allow you to notice what is going on around you as well as within you and your responses to it. By consciously attending in this way, the relationship between therapist and client deepens.

Pay attention from the moment the client walks through the door or you hear his or her voice on the phone. Notice as much as you can in detail as well as in a global way, like a camera lens moving in and out both toward the client and you. Noticing is an intuitive and artistic function that includes not only observation but reflection as well. When anyone approaches, there is an aura, a sense about them as they come through the door. So much is communicated in how a person walks, how they carry themselves, their gait, the pace with which they move, their confidence or hesitation. What are they wearing? Is it colorful or dull? Does it fit? Do they smile or convey ease? How do they find a seat? There are many cues that you pick up in a global way that contribute to answering the question of whether or not you and the client can or will choose to work together.

It is important that you ask yourself how you feel when sitting with a new client. What is awakened in you? Notice how the interaction left you. Were you saddened, irritated, or intrigued? Did you feel a sense of optimism that the relationship could be fruitful, or did the client talk so fast that it felt as though you had been caught in a blinding snowstorm? Were there so many traumatic memories revealed all at once that you were reeling inside, maybe feeling overwhelmed?

Checking in with yourself is crucial. What happened *for* you, the therapist?

When I am working, feelings move through me quite rapidly, as do thoughts and impressions. A client's story may touch off something familiar, or I may notice a mythic quality to their description and have a thought about that. For example, if the story describes disappointment and fruitless labor, I might think of Sisyphus pushing a rock up a mountain, or a mother's grief and distress may remind me of the myth of Demeter and Persephone. When these associations occur, I appreciate them, as they contribute information in a metaphoric manner. When thoughts and feelings coalesce, I move toward an image or idea of the client's dilemma. I am reminded of Pablo Picasso's description of his process in painting. He explains that when he begins to paint, an image seems to come forth from the canvas, as though it has a life of its own. Then he engages with it and co-creates it. Similarly, the client's story emerges and takes form as he or she speaks.

Several years ago a new client, Melissa, came to the office. She was in her late twenties, casually dressed, with short red hair. She described her dilemma as follows: "Sometimes I have an impulse to steal things, small things, mostly from the drug store," she explained. "I really don't know why I do it but I have been doing it since I was a teenager." She detailed many times in her life when the impulse to steal things had overtaken her, and offered her rationalizations and minimizations. I thought her impulses were particularly dangerous because she was a professional and the consequences of her actions could be dire.

Melissa's behavior seemed very much at odds with the rest of her hard-working and sincere presentation. When she described her compulsive behavior, I thought of how a person might tempt the fates, unconsciously. Was her behavior a way of treating her life like a roulette wheel, creating risk or possibly *re*creating it? After our first session, I thought about the Greek god Hermes, whom I associated with thievery and trickery. I wondered what unconscious motives were playing into Melissa's behavior, and what archetypes might be constellated. I decided to research Hermes a bit further.

Hermes was considered the messenger of the gods and also a "divine trickster." Wikipedia describes him as "the god of boundaries and the transgression of boundaries."[37] The more I read about this mercurial messenger the more I felt that Melissa was reenacting a trauma unconsciously. Where were the needed boundaries in her childhood? What had been stolen from her, taken thoughtlessly? Being able to see her theft as an attempt to resolve some terrible inner riddle helped me to have a bigger picture of her behavior. Then I understood that her theft, her transgression, was a key to opening her self-awareness. Hermes as messenger had brought a symptom that, when understood, contained a deeper resolution at a psychological/soulful level.

In the weeks that followed our session, I observed how such impulses arose in *me* when I was shopping, and how I dealt with them. I noticed my own feelings of temptation and desire. I watched my child self who "just wants it," and the adult self that sets the limit and says "no." I became curious about my client's unruly child self and recalled her description of her absent mother when she was young. In describing her early years, Melissa said that her mother had often left her in the care of other adults. She described times when she had been thrown back on her own instincts for survival. My image was of a baby left in a basket floating down the river, adrift. Who was in charge? Alcohol and drug use had played a part in her parents' lives together. Their marriage had been lengthy but unstable, with long periods of separation.

Melissa described many times when she had needed her mother's guidance and protection but her mother had been absent. She was often dropped off with neighbors for long periods of time. Her story was wrapped in tears and grief. I felt her helplessness and a pervasive sense of being lost in a grown-up world. Even so, she had chosen a career of service to others that required her to be very present.

I felt a tension in her, a kind of need to betray herself as *she* had been betrayed. Was stealing a way of calling out to her mother or father unconsciously to pay attention to her? Was the danger of being caught a kind of self-punishment, a way of expressing not being valuable enough to protect? Did risking everything make her feel more alive? I felt that I was looking at many facets of a crystal, exploring multiple possibilities.

As our conversations in sessions continued, it was clear to me that much of Melissa's behavior was tied to trauma. Tempting the fates had become a form of repetition compulsion. In my experience of countertransference, at times I felt the need to be the voice of the protective Mother. "Are you out of your mind?" I said to her one day. "Do you have any idea how dangerous this behavior is?" I wanted her to hear my feelings of concern in no uncertain terms. "I know," she replied quietly. I hoped that by my confronting her strongly, she would feel the depth of my caring and concern. We had many EMDR sessions (eye movement desensitization), which were very helpful in restoring her sense of control while dealing with the hurt and grief of childhood memories.

The work with Melissa lasted over three years. The consistency of our weekly meetings was reparative. Building a trusting and predictable relationship with the therapist was essential for her to cope with her feelings of betrayal by both parents. We explored the meaning of her shoplifting — her own form of betrayal and self-abandonment. Then, too, we considered her momentary thrill, a feeling of exaltation, similar to a child who feels that they have gotten away with something.

As Melissa worked in the sand tray, she was able to bring forth images that expressed how small and helpless she felt at times, as well as the anger that had been more covert but still present. Her work in the tray brought forth needed hope and imagination. After a year or so, she no longer felt the need to steal things. There was still much work to do, however, since taking things had been a symbolic action, a way of literalizing her impoverishment.

As the therapist, the trick in listening and staying present is not to edit your feelings and impressions because you think you should not have them or because you believe that you should be more objective. Absolutely not! You need *your* subjectivity, your capacity to be impressed or pressed upon. Through your engagement, the transference deepens. Without your vulnerability, there is not enough connection to do the work. So do not fear the feelings and ideas that may arise in you. Cherish them — because they all point to something important in the client and, of course, in you.

Discerning Pattern

There is a spiraled process in human activity that repeatedly takes us back to familiar places and leads to the possibility of increased awareness. The trick is to see through repeated behaviors in ways that ask different questions: "How is psyche/soul calling?" What gods reside in the action? "How can energy toward the sacred be made more conscious?"

As I write, it is a cool, grey day in February. When I walked in the garden this morning, I saw tall green shoots of Narcissus breaking through the hard earth. The pink camellias have begun to bloom cheerfully under the somber skies. They return so reliably every year in early spring, a harbinger of warmer and longer days to come. The repetitive patterns of nature anchor us. We humans rely on these cycles to know our place in the scheme of things. Similarly, we create patterns to locate ourselves in daily life, whether we are buying coffee in the morning or reading the newspaper.

I often awaken early, go into the kitchen, and make a pot of tea. I relish the familiar sound of water tumbling into the kettle and the sound of steam hissing as the water boils. Then I choose the teacup — simple or ornate, depending upon my mood. I sit in my studio, turn on the classical station, and drink a cup of tea. I gaze out of the window as the sun rises. This pattern is holy ground.

My initial training in recognizing patterns in human behavior came from watching soap operas as a kid. My parents both worked, and that left me home with our maid, Flo Flo, as I called her. We would sit and watch her favorite soaps, starting with *Search for Tomorrow*[38] and *The Guiding Light*.[39] I credit this early experience of watching daily storytelling with my later choice of career! The successful shows were archetypal; indeed, they *had* to be to capture and hold the audience in daily reverie. They touched on all of our human themes, our foibles and failures, as well as our excesses and successes. The soaps had it all — love and love lost, ego and hubris, deception and retribution, greed and hatred.

The beauty of these human dramas was also the daily rhythm of tuning in to them. They began with familiar music and, before you knew it, you were inducted into the family drama of your choice. Even as a young child I began to recognize patterns and gestures, as well as tone of voice and other cues. I intuited the presence and power of the unconscious, as characters made choices and decisions that inevitably led to disaster. Clearly, other aspects of the personality that were out of awareness, in shadow, had a part to play. Although at the time I did not have a vocabulary for what I was seeing, I did have an instinct or intuition.

A pattern can be as simple as driving on a particular route to work and doing it repeatedly, or carrying through a series of behaviors in the morning when we awaken. Patterns are part of nature's design, whether in a snowflake or in how a fish moves or in our thumbprint. In psychotherapy, our recognition and understanding of pattern as someone tells their story comes mostly from our ability to observe our *own* repetitive patterns. We notice specific actions and reactions, responses and cycles in our behavior over time. In this way, we discern that there is a spiraled process in human activity that takes us

Discerning Pattern

back again and again to the same places, ultimately leading to the possibility of increased awareness.

Awareness alone, however, is not a guarantee. Indeed, it seems that we humans frequently troll the same territory without waking up. The therapist's capacity to recognize pattern creates opportunities for her client to see what has been lying just under the surface and out of view. Freud named one of our more perplexing patterns the "repetition compulsion."[40] Why do we continue to make choices that lead repeatedly to the same undesirable results? Are we simply blind, or is there an unconscious need to revisit certain psychological territory until there is resolution? I opt for the latter possibility. Freud described this behavior as a process of "remembering, repeating, and working through." From a Jungian perspective, we are caught in a complex, reacting to unconscious stimuli. The stimulus is often traumatic. During this behavior we are split off from a more integrated awareness of our condition, like a lone rider in the wilderness. We are then compelled to act out our one-sided perception or attitude through repetitive patterns of behavior.

Repetition can be a gateway into a deeper reality through a connection to ritual. Some clients display patterns that we call "compulsive," such as repeatedly checking the stove and the lights or the door when leaving the house. These behaviors have a ritualistic quality. They provide a transition point between ordinary time and sacred time. I believe that these behaviors are an attempt to summon the gods for protection; they become a way to create a safe space, a kind of intermediary space between internal threats and outer symbolic gestures. As therapists, when we observe patterns of behavior in our clients that may seem deleterious, we need to observe respectfully and be curious as to the energy that underlies them and the meaning that the pattern carries for the individual.

How does a person change patterns that have become entrenched and are no longer productive? Often it requires a shock that makes the previous pattern less sustainable. The new element may be a difficulty, an illness, divorce, job loss, or some kind of shock that causes our usual, routine adaptations to fail. When a person is destabilized and at a point of crisis, they might consider entering therapy. They may know that *something needs to change*, but not necessarily how to change it.

Behavioral patterns or habits can create comfort, complacency, or frustration. Perhaps one of the most common complaints from clients is articulated in the phrase, "I feel stuck." When I hear this, I often wonder: "Stuck *in what*, and *how?*" I often suggest using art or sand tray to activate their imagination. "Can you *show* me how you are stuck?" I might ask, "What does it look like? What does it feel like? What color is it? How does being stuck feel in your body? Can you locate where you tighten? What images and associations surface as you begin to explore these feelings?" Sometimes, pulling gently on the somatic thread can lead to places that have been shut down because of trauma. Through the use of gentle movement, the body may begin to release feelings and images that have been buried.

I may ask the client to show me what "stuck" looks and feels like by using chalks, crayons, or colored pencils. Some years ago, Roger, a client in his sixties, described feelings of being "trapped," a similar problem. I offered him some pens and asked him to show me what that felt like. He chose a red pencil and drew a large rectangle. He said, "There is no way out." He emphasized the lines of the rectangle with the red pencil, repeating its quality of no exit.

Discerning Pattern

I pointed out that he did not draw *himself* inside the rectangle, as though the enclosure had all the power. He said that even being able to see himself in this way felt a bit more manageable. Within a minute or two, he became more engaged with the image and began to talk while drawing and emphasizing the red lines. I asked if he had any associations to this enclosure. Quite readily he recalled memories of being a child and feeling trapped. He had been hospitalized as a very young child, three or four, with gastrointestinal problems. At that time, his parents had not been allowed to stay with him in the hospital, and were constrained by strict visiting schedules. Roger had impressions of a green room and his own terrible feelings of isolation, fear, and abandonment. In my experience, hospitalizations and surgeries for children — and for adults, as well — are very frightening and traumatic. Often, details of the incident have slipped away into the unconscious but they have left a distinct emotional trail.

Roger was clearly sad and distraught as he engaged with these memories. He kept drawing and emphasizing the lines that held him trapped. Ironically, by doing this, he began to experience a hint of control over his prison. As he continued to draw, he said that the box felt less solid. He created a small opening in the bottom left-hand corner. He said that, previously, he did not think there could be any opening. Now the enclosure felt more permeable.

Over several weeks he continued to work with the image through active imagination. Just as in a dream, Roger began to understand that he was playing all the parts in the image: he was both the container and the prisoner. In future sessions, he began to investigate the box. His desire to be free increased, as did the size of the opening at the corner of the box. Now there was more information flowing through the portal to the unconscious, and into his outer world as well.

Roger connected to his intuitive faculty in conversation with the image. He verbalized more emotions and had a growing sense of freedom. His container had held him in and held him back. At the same time, it had served to protect him from a world that felt dangerous and threatening.

Because of the traumatic nature of Roger's experience, I also used EMDR, or Eye Movement Desensitization Reprogramming, a highly effective treatment for PTSD developed by Francine Shapiro.[41] Using EMDR served to lessen Roger's anxiety and allowed him to have a more positive outlook on life. He understood that the container had been like a chrysalis that had held him for a time and now no longer served him.

I asked about the effect of his changed outlook on his relationship with his girlfriend. He told me that they had taken a trip together and had a "great" time. He smiled more, and his sense of humor began to emerge. Roger was in treatment for several years. His emotions were still, at times, problematic, but now they were accessible and he could work with them.

Another common complaint from clients also suggests unconscious repetition. Someone will say, "I feel like I am hitting the wall." When I hear this, I ask the client to *show* me the wall. I provide pens, pencils, chalks, and oil pastels. "What is the wall made of?" I wonder. "How thick is it? How do you see yourself in relationship to it?" I wonder what is being walled in and what is being walled off. When the client draws the wall or creates it with clay, memories and associations may follow. We use the image to stir the imagination, to invite psyche to come forward. I often wonder, "Where are the hidden figures? What or who is behind the wall?" The image acts as a window into the unconscious.

Inquiry can take many forms, but once feelings are evoked, a client may begin to feel unburdened, relieved of something that has weighed them down for a long time. By engaging the client's own intuition, the meaning of the image may reveal itself. In this way the feeling of "stuckness" potentially thins and dissolves. Jung wrote that "the primary function of intuition, however, is to transmit images, or perceptions or relations between things; which could not be transmitted by the other functions or only in a very roundabout way. These images have the value of specific insights which have a decisive influence on action whenever intuition is given priority.[42]

Patterns that habitually repeat may have varied meanings and wear different faces. For example, a pattern can wear the face of addiction and compulsion, an unconscious and destructive face. Or patterning can be a road to excellence, as in practicing a musical instrument or performing stretches and positions at the *barre* in ballet. Repetition also has a place in spiritual practice, where ritual prayer and meditation play an integral part in creating and sustaining experience. Coming weekly to see a therapist is also an intentional ritual where time is set aside for self-revelation and healing. The meaning of a specific pattern or ritual can be investigated and made more conscious.

The trick is to see through repeated behaviors in ways that ask different kinds of questions: "How is psyche/soul calling?" "Whom does it serve?" "What gods reside in the action?" These questions move away from what is a purely literal description of the behavior and, instead, consider how energy is being used and toward what end.

Symptom as Messenger

Like patterns, symptoms, too, ask for our awareness. They ask us to allow them to live in image and metaphor so that we can better understand aspects of the self that need attention. Why have they come? What are they trying to tell us? We assume they have arrived for good cause.

Through my studies at Pacifica Graduate Institute, I encountered the work of James Hillman, a brilliant psychologist and guide to psyche. Hillman revisited most of the assumptions upon which modern psychology is based. He turned them upside down and inside out to better see through to a deeper knowing. He opened up an amazing conversation, a way of understanding the nature of symptom and illness as expressions of soul. Hillman writes:

> Before any attempt to treat, or even understand, pathologized phenomena, we meet them as an act of faith, regarding them as authentic, real, and valuable as they are. We do not decrease their value by considering them as signs of medical sickness or inflate their value by considering them as signs of spiritual suffering. They are ways of the psyche and ways of finding soul.[43]

What does it mean to hold the symptom as "authentic, real, and valuable" without attempting to change it in any way? Hillman suggests that we allow the Hermetic nature of the symptom to express itself just as it is. In psychology, we are often asked to mitigate the symptoms, to bring relief, to instigate a program of change. Thus, to pause and accept what is, without forcing or manipulating a change, is a very different way of holding psychological material. We might consider that psyche has gone to great trouble to find the perfect symptom to express the distress of soul; therefore, let us attend and encourage the client to receive the communication that is being delivered in the form of a symptom. Engaging the symptom as image takes the client on a soulful journey to a deeper and more meaningful aspect of him- or herself.

Let us imagine that psyche sends a symptom to awaken the client to an illness of soul. Delivered by Hermes, the messenger of the gods, the symptom carries its own truth. Holding the symptom in this way is close to how the Greeks first conceived of disease — not as an isolated problem but rather as something that pointed to an imbalance in the whole personality and body. Healing was a complex process that included treating the whole person on many levels — through rest, dreams, humor, and catharsis. As a therapist, the word "soul" may or may not be in your working vocabulary, and it certainly is not in the *DSM-5*[44]; and yet, as clinicians, we are asked to consider the diagnosis, to name it, and to cure it. How do we walk this path?

I think of a diagnosis as a *description with many different attributes*. The dictionary adds some nuance, saying that it is a "condition," a "system or approach," a "road," or even a "custom."[45] Depression, for example, has many faces. It is not a singular entity but a composite of feeling, gesture, posture, tone, biology, and so forth. It is a palpable presence, a character in its own right. I often ask, "Whom does it serve, and why has it come to visit *at this time*?"

When I was working with children, many parents came to see me to ask if their child had ADHD. It is a relatively new yet pervasive diagnosis, a description of certain behaviors that describe difficulty in attending in a focused manner.

We know that these behaviors can be very difficult for the child and parents. However, is it possible to honor the child's process and not see it *only* as a problem or a diagnosis to be cured? I used to ask the children whom I saw in therapy what they were thinking when they were looking out the window in class and not attending to the teacher. "Where did you *want* to put your attention?" I might say. I was curious about focusing, itself — what was included and what was excluded in order to focus? In this way, I was trying to understand the context of the symptom and its presence in the child's life. In other words, what does it mean that soul finds expression through illness, and what is being communicated?

When working with children, I always offered use of the sand tray as a means to express themselves. Most children, even those diagnosed with ADD or ADHD, were able to concentrate as they played in the sand. Their more erratic and unfocused behavior abated and they could concentrate more easily. They often chatted as they created, describing their process. Of course, working one-to-one, rather than in a classroom with thirty children, made it possible for them to function with less distraction. They were able to say things that were not easily spoken under normal circumstances.

As they played in the sand, they often described their frustrations at school and home. It hurt not to be like other kids, not to be normal. They told me about having to sit in special seats in the classroom or having to stay in at recess because of their behavior. These conversations revealed deep feelings of sadness and shame. By listening empathically to the child's story, we developed a trusting relationship that opened up possibilities for helping them to suffer less. I also had family sessions where I inquired into family history and dynamics. Often the dad or close relative had had a similar profile of restlessness and difficulty in school. Quite often they had forgotten about it or buried it, along with their own shame. Then, as I worked with the whole family, we could look at the issues of behavior, frustration, and failure systemically, thus moving the child out of the role of identified patient. ADD and ADHD are diagnoses about which we are still learning a great deal. The *function of the symptom*, however, remains a very important question as we continue to investigate these behaviors. What else may be at play when a person is easily distracted or unable to attend? I often found, in my work with abuse and trauma victims, symptoms that mimicked ADHD but had a different source.

Symptoms are like actors upon a stage; therefore, it behooves us to know the plot. As therapists, we need to pay attention to the symptoms as messengers from the unconscious with a tale to tell. If we move too quickly to solve the problem, as we are often instructed to do under managed care, we may miss important information and context that has to do with the message contained within the symptom.

For example, consider this familiar scene. Your client comes into the session looking frazzled. She puts her hand briefly to her forehead and mentions that she has a headache. At this point, you have several choices. You can empathize and offer her some ibuprofen, or you can begin to bring a different kind of attention to her symptoms. Typically, I bring out a pad of paper and ask the client to *draw* the headache, bringing it directly and deliberately into the room and the conversation. Usually, this suggestion is met with some curiosity on the client's part.

As she works, I notice the colors she chooses, the medium (pencil, chalk, pen, or crayon), and the intensity or timidity with which she draws. Once she has created the image, we can begin to expand on it. "How do you feel about what you have created?" I ask. "What was it like for you to give expression to your pain?" Notice that I am not asking directly about the meaning of the symptom, but rather how the client feels about engaging with it. Sometimes these questions elicit pertinent responses and even strong emotions. Now you can be curious *together* about the qualities of the headache, what it evokes in the client, and how it arrives with a message to deliver. One could consider this whole process an intuitive exploration as client and therapist work to elicit the soulfulness of the symptom.

Following this line of inquiry soon makes it clear that the headache is not an arbitrary event but a symptom intimately connected to the matter at hand. The client might wonder what she is trying to resolve mentally that might ask for a different kind of solution: "How do I respond to pressure? What is the nature of this pressure, and how familiar is it? What is being pressed down or pressed upon within me? How does the body/mind communicate who suffers?" In no way do you want to make the headache wrong. Instead, encourage an empathic response to the image, one of curiosity and openness, if possible.

Symptoms ask for attention. They ask to live through image and metaphor in order for us to understand who or what in us needs to be heard. Perhaps the inquiry, itself, becomes a soulful exploration. In my personal lexicon soul is not a place but rather a qualitative experience or even a creative urge. Soul feels resonant, wet, beautiful, grieving, mutable, dark, and ephemeral.

As professionals, when a client's symptoms are life threatening, we are required to take action in certain ways to keep the client safe; and, of course, we do. We are concerned about their well-being and all that entails. At the same time, we want to consider: in what way does this crisis bring needed attention? "Who calls?" psychologically speaking.

Now, as a Jewish mother, I take physical and mental issues very seriously. "So, have you seen a doctor?" I ask the client. I say this to assure you that I am not at all indifferent to physical pain and suffering. I keep a dual vision. For example, when a person is depressed, by all means encourage them to have their thyroid checked. I always do. I encourage the client to see a physician to discover physical causes that might be contributing to the patient's distress. When it seems warranted, I may suggest a consult for medication. All symptoms are connected to each other and to the totality of a person. By attending to symptoms physically, emotionally, and imaginally, we invite in a bigger picture.

To understand how a person has become who they are is to recognize how they have attempted to heal themselves many times over, even though they may still be suffering acutely. Paying attention in this way honors each person's desire to right themselves like a ship in a storm. Staying open to hearing all of the voices speaking through symptom allows the messenger to deliver his soulful tale.

Creativity and Addiction

> *Addiction obscures spiritual impulses and substitutes a substance for what is, in fact, truly substantive and of the soul. It occurs to me that creativity and intuition spring from the same invisible source. Thus both have a partially hidden or obscured nature, and neither is under the control of the ego. Rather, both seem to operate from a hidden source. We can only create opportunities for their appearance.*

Making opportunities for creative expression in the therapeutic relationship initiates a powerful healing force. The therapist learns to ask different questions of the process: for example, "How can we understand addiction through a metaphoric lens? How is psyche/soul calling? How can energy toward the sacred be made more conscious?" Asking these kinds of questions leads to opportunities for the client to express and release feelings in a new way, through creative expression. It also invites in the gods, a spiritual summons, since the nature of addiction and compulsion at one level is about power, control, and ego.

The invitation to express one's feelings and images that issue from the unconscious is a summons to spirit. Addiction obscures spiritual impulses and substitutes a substance for what is, in fact, truly substantive and of the soul. When this occurs, an addict often feels trapped and unable to see through his behavior. Linda Leonard suggests, in her book, *Witness to the Fire: Creativity and the Veil of Addiction*,[46] that creative expression invites a very different approach to a difficult problem. Linda Leonard's book shaped my thinking about addiction and how to work with it. Her focus is on how addiction derails the creative impulse and substitutes alcohol or other drugs and spirits for the actual experience of creativity. I have had many clients who recall abandoning their creativity and substituting drinking or gambling or other compulsive behaviors for more internally driven expression. Leonard asks: Who are the gods behind the veil, and how can a person work toward recovery, from a spiritual and creative perspective?

Building on Leonard's work, I find that following a line of inquiry that includes a client's creative life can be revealing. When taking a history, I often ask if the client has ever been interested in art, music, or poetry. Have they ever thought of themselves as creative or artistic? This question often solicits poignant and meaningful responses. Sometimes a client seems surprised, even ashamed or embarrassed. Unfortunately, many people begin with an apology or explanation for how they gave up the creative part of themselves. They describe a betrayal of something very deep inside of them. I have heard many stories of cruel remarks by a teacher or parent about a child's drawing or handwriting, and the devastating consequences of these remarks. Often the child makes a decision, right then and there, not to go down the path of creative expression again. These terrible stories move me deeply, as I feel that something very precious and soulful has been robbed from them and subsequently buried. At the same time, I am hopeful that, through our work, their creative impulse will be reawakened.

This was the case with John, a man in his early forties who had come to therapy complaining of depression. He began his life's story by saying that in his teens, he had begun drinking and had never stopped. He was now in AA and attending meetings several times a week. He told me that his father was an abusive alcoholic and that he had not seen him for over ten years.

John presented in a very sensitive way, speaking softly, almost apologetically. He was ashamed of his drinking and had tried to stop many times. He felt that it had derailed his life. I asked, "How is this so? What has drinking prevented you from doing?" He told me that, as a young boy, he had been interested in art. He had carved totem poles and even created a collection of them. He had been interested in painting and pottery, as well, but his father had been disparaging and dismissive of his talent. He had turned away from these sensibilities in himself.

"Do you ever feel the urge to do creative work now?" I asked.

"No," he replied wistfully. "That was a long time ago."

At my suggestion, John began working with the sand tray almost immediately. It was clear that he enjoyed the process and felt comfortable moving the sand and using the figures. On one particular afternoon, he approached the shelves thoughtfully. He chose the totem pole and placed it in the center of the tray. It stood alone, a tall, solitary presence. It was a powerful statement. After he had completed the tray, we both stood and looked at it silently, reverently. The totem pole felt to me like John's sacred spirit reaching to the sky. John looked pleased with his creation. I gave him a photo of it and asked him to look at it several times during the week. He smiled and agreed.

Over time, John made increasingly elaborate scenes of his childhood and of Native Americans and their arts, and it was clear that this expression gave him joy. At the same time, he began to talk about his heritage and the ways in which his creativity had been a source of fulfillment for him when he was young. He felt that as a young adult he had lost his spiritual anchor and that he had betrayed something very deep within himself.

Alcoholism had only increased John's feelings of emptiness and lack of purpose. In time, John was able to talk about his childhood and the deep feelings of sadness and loss that he felt. As he worked in the sand, he recalled many people and places that had meaning for him. He loved his grandparents and felt shame about how he had disappointed them. At the same time, his process of recollection and retrieval seemed to stir something powerful inside him. His need and desire to express his feelings found a way through the sand medium of the tray. Several months later, he brought in a small figure of a boy that he had carved. Working with his hands began to bring him joy and purpose once again. He was able to maintain sobriety through Alcoholics Anonymous, psychotherapy, and his own creative work. Working with John was a great pleasure for me. It was very fulfilling to watch and support his creative life.

At the core of addiction is often undiagnosed depression. I learned many years ago that a definition of depression is that it is also a lack of imagination. When a person cannot imagine any circumstance as different from what is before them, they cannot move toward a solution or alternative. Playing in the sand and water of the sand tray invites imagination. The opportunity to create, activates the unconscious and opens the gates to resources that have been out of awareness and out of reach. The safety of working in the sand with a therapist as a witness rests in the silence of the process. The client is supported and seen, and yet there is no verbal comment or distraction. The client operates in a safe container, free to express whatever he/she chooses.

Creativity and Addiction

I find that working with addiction is very challenging. Usually, it is a lengthy process and a very spiraled journey, with many twists and turns. Alcoholism and depression usually require a many-pronged approach that includes depth work, family therapy, alleviating PTSD, and the support of Alcoholics Anonymous. In addition, I find that seeing the healing process through the lens of creativity and creative potential enhances the work. Working with a person who suffers from addiction asks me to see through to what is underneath the behavior, to all that has been abandoned and also to all that has been unlived. As Linda Leonard suggests, addiction is a veil that obscures the soul shimmering behind it. Our work and challenge is to address that presence.

Sitting with Loss

The therapeutic container acts as a vessel for grief and loss. By attending to your pain, the alchemy of suffering turns to gold.

The experience of loss frequently motivates clients to seek counseling, although they may not recognize that loss, itself, is the issue. One might say that the therapist acts as an undertaker, the one who guides and accompanies the client through a descent and across the great water to the land of the dead. My understanding and appreciation for this perspective came from Robert Romanyshyn, my professor at Pacifica Graduate Institute, who lectured on psyche-centered therapy. The landscape of grieving, "work at the gravesite of loss," is at the core of psyche-centered therapy, which counsels "fidelity to the perspective of soul."[47] Through the process of grieving, the client works to recover images that ask to be honored and finally put to rest. During the time I took this deeply moving and powerful class, I worked with a young woman in her thirties whom we will call Elaine. The following is a description of our process.

Elaine and I sat quietly, at first, taking each other in.

"Where to begin?" she asked.

"Anywhere," I suggested. "We have time." And so the journey began.

She told her story in a southern drawl — North Carolina, as it turned out. As she spoke, the therapy room expanded to include a sentient southern landscape whose history and images breathed life into her story. Her recollections reached back into childhood, to the small town where she had lived with her parents and four younger siblings, all close in age.

"I was the oldest," she explained. "That meant a lot of responsibility, cooking, cleaning, and caring for the little ones."

As she spoke, I could almost smell the scent of the kitchen, the wood-burning stove, and the sounds of children. Her voice was full of emotion as she thought of her mother, who was over-burdened and depressed. Her father was hard-working but said very little. "He tried his best," she explained.

She was proud of her mother's ingenuity in getting the needs of the children met. Her eyes were soft as she described her early years.

She told me about her first marriage coming apart in mid-life. There were children who had been left behind, and a searing pain left unhealed. She stopped talking as tears came. I saw around her the wisps of a wedding veil, belying the innocence of her expectation and the virginal quality of her hope. Her voice was sad, like the notes of a cello, as she spoke of her disappointment. As she continued talking, the geography shifted to her current life. She had moved to California, far away from her parents and her youth, and into her second marriage. She seemed like a plant that had been uprooted and was still in shock. The new birth that she had imagined and hoped for, unencumbered by the ghosts of her past, had not materialized. Instead, she found herself full of doubts and fear as unmourned places in psyche called for her attention.

I felt as though she needed to cry and grieve desperately. Our first few sessions revealed more details of her losses and the difficult decisions she had made. I felt that I was there to receive, hold, and witness her. It was clear that guilt and shame plagued her. Her first marriage had been very difficult: her husband had been much like her father, strict and taciturn. After twenty years of struggle, she had left him and the children as well.

In our early sessions, our conversation shuttled between past and present. I worked like a painter, curious about negative space — the part of a painting that is in the background but holds and contains what is in the foreground. Our work focused on Elaine's reconnection to her younger self, the woman she had been, her hopes and dreams, and the harsh realities she had encountered. The nature of her grieving came to include extending kindness and compassion toward herself in present time, as well as toward the young, idealistic woman she had been.

Our work together resurrected images of her youth, her parents, siblings, aunts, uncles, and ancestors, particularly the women in her family. What had they dreamed of doing with their lives? What had her *mother* wanted? What idea of self had been passed onto her like a baton in a relay race? What in her past remained unfinished and unmourned, and how was this influencing her life now? Over time, she began to understand that many of her choices had been shaped by influences of which she had been unaware and over which she had no control.

When we worked on issues of past loss and grief, the sessions went well. However, if I digressed and asked about her current marriage or some other "problem" that she needed to deal with, everything came to a grinding halt. I noticed that when we fell out of metaphor and into the literal, everything shifted, and she became reticent and reluctant. I needed to follow her lead. I came to realize that Elaine was telling me in different ways that she was not ready to deal with certain things in her present.

Between sessions, I found myself feeling that she was not going to come back. She changed appointments frequently and came on a bi-weekly basis, insisting that she had too much work to do. When she did return, I found myself surprised. Where did these feelings come from in *me*? I noticed my own feelings of rejection and doubt tied to my childhood.

After several months, I told Elaine about my feelings of discomfort. I sensed a block or wall between us, even though on the surface everything looked okay. By going into my own body, I sensed the presence of something I could not put my finger on.

I asked, "When I speak to you, can you feel my words enter you?"

"No," she said. "They are about out to here," gesturing to a place about an arm's length from her body.

She is "keeping me at arm's length"! I thought. Her telling me this was a great relief, a confirmation of my uneasiness.

Then she said, "I don't want to deal with this new marriage quite yet. I know that I will when I am ready."

I was relieved. I could relax. We both could. We did not have to hold up the tent of "therapy" as a concept; instead, we could allow something real to live between us. Maybe now Elaine would not need the wall. Acknowledging my discomfort allowed her to be angry with me, in her own polite way. It also allowed me to make a space for her disappointment to enter our conversation.

"Well, what shall we do now?" I asked playfully.

"You mean, we don't have to work on anything?" she asked.

"Nope," I said whimsically. "Maybe next time, let's play."

Suddenly she burst out crying. This was the most emotion she had displayed in our time together. This moment reminded me of "reflexio," a term used by James Hillman to describe a moment of wonder "initiated by the soul."[48] This experience interrupts one's normal perception, like a crack in a mirror through which we see into a different reality. The absence of play between us and in her life was clear. The "work" of therapy had been, at times for her, just that — only more work.

Now there was an opening into her grief. Here was a woman who had tried so hard to be a good daughter, a good mother, and a good wife that all the play and joy of life had gone out of her. I had been, in a sense, infected by her belief that life was difficult. I had fallen into being a "good" therapist and imagining that I could take away her pain through work and persistence. By trying to assuage her despair, I had almost lost her. When I let go, the creative energy in her came forth to find its own way. In the next session I brought in a large block of clay.

"Are we going to play with that?" she asked, a capricious, childlike grin crossing her face. As we talked, her hands moved happily, folding and molding, seemingly with their own purpose. She created a feminine presence wearing a cloak.

"She is an angel," Elaine said. It was clear that she was very moved by this figure.

Curiously enough, as Elaine molded the clay, she talked about her current marriage and her own process in dealing with it. I listened, saying very little. My silence was a gesture toward her. Without my probing or prompting, she felt free to express herself in her own way.

I saw her only one more time after this session. The next time she came in, she talked about her daughter and their relationship. I mentioned doing a sand tray or returning to the clay, but she was not interested. At the end of the session, she informed me that she would be working full time for one month and that she would call me after that. I knew in that moment that she would not return. I had a sinking feeling in my stomach.

Once again, work was cast as the villain. I believe the breakthrough that had taken place was too much for her. Once she had opened into the imaginal realm, she had an opportunity to face her losses creatively in a way that might have rendered the deepest healing; but she was not ready. I had to honor that, as I struggled with my own emotional investment in the relationship. Elaine helped me to understand that each person grieves in her own way and her own time. The process cannot be hurried. By *following* her instead of trying to lead, I could be there if and when she decided to turn around.

Grief work is very profound and part of almost any therapeutic process. Each person grieves for what they have lost or never known, what they have imagined to be so and what is not. Grief is a vehicle for touching deeply into life itself.

When I first encountered Mogenson's work on grief in *Greeting the Angels: An Imaginal View of the Mourning Process*, I felt a deep comfort, a salve, a soothing balm. He writes:

> From the imaginal point of view, the end of life is not the end of soul. The images continue.... The psyche is created, in large measure, by the mourning process itself. The more precisely we imagine our losses, the more psychological we become. We are the afterworld in which our loved ones dwell. It is not simply that *they* live on in us; *we* live on in them as well.[49]

Later in his book, he writes: "The dark impulses which guide creative work are of a kind with the impulses that compel the work of mourning. Just like the artist or writer who sits down to work without knowing in advance exactly what his labors will give birth to, we mourn in suspense the autonomy of the image."[50]

After reading Mogenson's book, I felt compelled to write. I imagined myself walking through a graveyard of souls where frozen ideas were melting and dissolving, dragging behind me like an old nightshirt, still attached and thinning. Then new images emerged that felt as tender as new skin beginning to knit over a cut, as determined as new shoots among hollow stalks. Angels called me to feel the wings of their presence, asking me to listen and trust that all things awaken us for the sake of soul. As I consider this, I think that all things arrive for a purpose, and that our work is to make meaning of our lives.

Curiouser and Curiouser

When you are sitting with your client, stay in the mystery, in the "I don't know" place; allow your curiosity to lead you. Follow your nose, little hare.

Today, I was sitting with a new client. As I reflected on our process, I saw that I was following my curiosity and allowing it to lead me. Perhaps you recall the white rabbit in *Alice in Wonderland*? Alice is sitting at a picnic, rather bored, until she sees a white rabbit looking at his pocket-watch as he runs by, saying, "Oh dear, oh dear! I shall be too late!" Without thinking, Alice jumps to her feet and runs off after it. She is just in time to see it pop down a large rabbit hole under the hedge. In another moment, down goes Alice after it, never once considering how in the world she is to get out again.[51] Alice, of course, follows the rabbit into a whole new world of experience.

Here is an example of how curiosity ignites intuition and guides the psychotherapy dialogue.

Lola sat quietly contained in her chair. Her eyes peeked out from lowered lids. Perhaps it was my imagination, but I felt that *she* was curious, too. An unusual question came to my mind: "How do you spend your days?" I asked her. "What occupies you?"

"I am a musician," she offered. I was surprised, as her demeanor was so subdued.

"What instrument do you play?" I asked. I could feel a little excitement bubbling up in me.

"The horn," she said quietly.

"Wow, interesting choice," I said with enthusiasm. My response was spontaneous and in contrast to her own. I imagined the horn, a large golden orb with bold sounds coming out of it, in contrast to the rather quiet and understated woman sitting in front of me. My own early memories of playing the violin and the piano floated through my mind.

«What made you choose the horn?» I asked, intrigued.

"My father liked it," she answered, "but I did, too." Her family thread presented itself, but I chose not to follow it just yet. Music was an important thread in Lola's story, as was making sound. Her voice barely audible, at times, was swallowed up by her self-disclosed depression — a small voice that wanted to be bigger. I found myself leaning toward her as she spoke. My mind went into a brief memory of a writing class I had once attended, in which I drew the word "horn" out of a basket and had to write about it. The gist of my writing was the phrase "blowing your own horn." Apt, I thought.

"It's difficult to be in situations with new people and to know what to say," she explained. "Sometimes they just lose interest and walk away." I could feel the depth of loneliness and despair resounding in her. I paused briefly and took a breath, feeling the portent of her words: her voice had become truncated and silenced.

"Is this an old experience for you, something from your family, perhaps?" I inquired.

She nodded her head yes, and mumbled something about her brothers and being overridden, even though she was the oldest. I watched her intently. I noticed that I was very still and that she, too, barely moved in the chair, her hands resting in her lap. Nonetheless, she answered my questions willingly, unfolding aspects of her life.

"Do you want to ask me anything?" I offered.

"No," she replied.

I waited. I felt quiet and focused. As I watched her, I felt a sense of mystery about her. I had no plan, nothing I could have articulated as such; and yet my questions and her responses seemed to make a kind of word-bridge between us. There was a rhythm, soft and gentle, call-and-response, nothing brash. Where or how this would all go, I did not know. Then, surprisingly, she asked me about the sand tray figures and what they were for. I was pleased that she was curious, and I explained their purpose.

"Would you like to choose something?" I asked.

She got up from her chair and went purposefully to a small yellow canoe. She placed it in the lower right-hand corner of the tray, and then returned quickly to her chair.

"Let's look at the tray together," I suggested. We got up and stood in front of the tray in silence. She seemed pleased. I waited a bit and then asked, "How was that for you?"

"I liked it," she said. I thanked her for taking the risk. I felt certain that our journey had begun.

Sitting with Lola, I sensed filings coming to the magnet in an intuitive way. My questions and her responses seemed to bring forth images and feelings that might soon create a path for her to follow. I liked her and hoped that in time she would find her own horn and blow it however she needed to.

The Gift of Sand and Water

"The psyche has an inherent tendency to heal itself; the task is given to the therapist to prepare the path for this tendency." [52]
— Dora Kalff

I was 35 years old and in therapy for the first time. My marriage had ended. I was now a single mother with two children. My therapist had a sand tray in her office and shelves filled with miniature figures of all kinds. The sand tray is a wooden box of specific dimensions filled with sand. She suggested that I allow myself to play with the sand and the figures, enjoying their texture and presence. I could create a scene or picture or not. Whatever I chose to do was fine. She also explained that this process was best done in silence. She sat nearby and gently observed.

My fingers moved noiselessly through the white sand, making whirls and spirals. I mounded the sand up on one side of the tray, then moved it over to the other side. I dug down to the bottom of the sand tray and found a blue bottom suggestive of the ocean. Then my eyes turned toward the shelves with myriad figures. I no longer remember what I chose that first day, but I do recall the feeling of delight and expectation that accompanied my search. I knew immediately and intuitively that the figures carried symbolic meaning, and I was intrigued. When I had finished, she took a picture of the tray that I had made with a Polaroid camera, handed it to me, and suggested that I keep it. This was the beginning of my love affair with sand tray therapy.

The trays felt like dreams and seemed to mirror and reflect my circumstances, although not in a literal way. At the same time, the tactile experience of my hands in the sand, building and creating symbolic worlds, was new and different from my more intellectual tendencies. The metaphoric process was creative and enlivening. I found that I could express and visualize aspects of myself that were hard to access in other ways. The trays seemed to progress, to have a kind of rhythm that intrigued me. Some were about familiar content, while others touched into spiritual feelings and mystery. When I worked in the sand I often felt that I was on a journey from one place to another. I sensed an inner movement, both in terms of depth and breadth.

I entered graduate school six months later to become a Marriage and Family Therapist. There, I encountered and was deeply moved by the work of Dora Kalff, a Jungian analyst in Switzerland who worked with children using the sand tray. She described how imaginal play touched deeply and gently into the unconscious, propitiating healing. I found her book, *Sandplay: A Psychotherapeutic Approach to Psyche*,[53] inspiring and motivating. I began studying and reading as much as I could about her way of working with children. Her approach felt loving, wise, and effective and I was very drawn to it as a way to do therapy.

I was never fortunate enough to meet Dora Kalff in person. I registered for a conference with her here in the United States but she became ill and it was cancelled. Nonetheless, her way of working has guided me all these years and I am deeply grateful to her. In her book there is a picture of her home in Switzerland. Her house had a beautiful door and a welcoming presence. I was so moved by the image that I have always had my office in my home, or (as with my last office) just across the driveway. In her book she writes:

The Gift of Sand and Water

> The children who come to see me for treatment suffer mostly from lack of inner security; they have no feeling of belonging. Something prevents the normal growth which is necessary for their inner balance. It may be an unfavorable home or outside the home situation. Because of this, I believe that it is very important not to separate the place of my practice from the environment and atmosphere of my home where it occurs.[54]

I believe that this description by Kalff touched the child in me who felt, at times, homeless.

I discovered how deeply healing the sand tray could be when I worked with sexually abused children and their families at Tulare Youth Services, an agency in the Central Valley of California. Most of the children took to the process with delight and enthusiasm. I was able to witness how effectively the tray held their deep emotion and at the same time created opportunities for healing and growth. It was clear that play activated their imaginations and opened up their own resources. I felt inspired and grateful to be a part of so many healing journeys. When children play in the sand, they tend to talk and move around a lot. They are more active than adults, who are often quiet and thoughtful. I have many pictures of children who, when they finished their trays, loved having Polaroid pictures of themselves with their creations. They felt so much pride and joy in what they had accomplished.

In sand tray therapy the therapist sits in silence as a child or adult plays in the sand. She witnesses their work in an unspoken way that communicates to them how much she values their work. She watches and attends with the eyes of a loving mother. As I attend to the client, I notice not only what figures they choose to place in the tray but how they move, their body language, and their attitude. Are they confident or hesitant, hurried or patient? As they create the tray, I am also aware of my own responses and thoughts, but I am not in an analytical mode. I want to be present to the client's process and also aware of the images as they unfold.

In sand tray therapy, the therapist is asked not to "do" in the traditional sense. Instead, she needs to hold the space, trust the process, and provide a safe container and appropriate boundaries for the work. She needs to be authentic in her responses and aware of her own internal reactions. When a child or adult asks for feedback about the tray, it is best to make general responses about their effort and concentration rather than offering an opinion or interpretation about specifics of the tray. In this way, the client is encouraged to continue in their process safely without direction or judgment from the therapist. Whatever the child or adult does in the tray is accepted fully and received lovingly.

Even now, many years later, my heart leaps when a client feels drawn to look at the shelves and peruse the figures; when they are willing to take the chance to put something in the sand and express themselves. I am never bored when clients work in the sand. I am, in fact, intrigued, curious, and delighted. I am also relieved, because I know that this very special engagement with the elements in the sand moves the therapy forward in a safe and depthful manner. Watching someone taking the risk to create is a privilege. I believe that psyche/soul is present to whatever occurs.

When a client's imagination is engaged in symbolic play, an opening into unconscious and transformative material takes place. The client transitions from a literal understanding of her distress into a place where metaphor and symbol inform her in a deeper way.

The Gift of Sand and Water

In his own life, C. G. Jung discovered the magic of sand and water at a time when he was in great emotional distress: his relationship with his mentor, Sigmund Freud, had ended in an unhappy way. They had diverged strongly in their interpretations of the unconscious, and Jung had left, determined to develop his own theories on the collective unconscious.

Nonetheless, Jung was devastated by the loss of the relationship and soon found himself lost in depression. In his autobiography, he described how he would play in a stream near his home, allowing himself to build with water and stone just as he had when he was a young child. He wrote in his memoir: "I asked myself, Now really, what are you about? You are building a small town, and doing it as if it were a rite! I had no answer to my question, only the inner certainty that I was on the way to discovering my own myth."[55] Shortly thereafter, his depression lifted and he returned to his work enlivened.

The archetypal/metaphoric experience of sand tray therapy is an entrance into psyche that propitiates healing. Kalff wrote: "The psyche has an inherent tendency to heal itself. The task is given to the therapist to prepare the path for the tendency."[56] The use of the tray is integral to my work and I trust it implicitly. If you have the opportunity to work in this way in your own therapy, you will know the transformative power of this deep and silent work.

If the sand tray calls to you, please do your own therapeutic work with it. Study, be curious, and follow your instincts. Buy or make a tray and begin to collect miniatures. Make trays at all times of the day and night, and see what comes to you. As you play, notice the figures that you include, the way you feel about them, how and where you place them in the tray, and the feelings that the process evokes in you. Look up symbols, and read myths and fairy tales. Follow your nose; sniff things out like a hare in the garden! In this way you will enter the depth and beauty of this work through your own experience and curiosity. Then, if you feel that this form of inquiry and creative expression serves you, find a therapist experienced with sand tray work who will witness your process in the sand. In this way, you will benefit most fully from this soulful journey.

Playing All 88 Keys

We are inclined to repeat old notes and play familiar tunes. The trick is to move out of familiar territory and make new alliances.

As a young child, I opened the door to the basement in Uncle Dave's house, cautiously feeling the sudden shift in temperature and a sense of opening into something mysterious and even a little dangerous. I reached for the overhead light as I descended the steep stairs. At the bottom was a huge black upright piano that loomed over me. I pulled myself up onto the round, hard wooden stool and banged away for hours, enchanted with the sounds that I could make.

By contrast, in Aunt Helene's house, a polished spinet piano sat proudly in the living room. It was shiny mahogany with a refined tone, unlike the old upright at Uncle Dave's house. The keys were smooth and easy. None of them had broken ivory that looked like chipped teeth, and when you struck the keys they didn't make that funny reverberating sound. I could not reach the pedals on either piano unless I stood up and played at the same time. I had to walk to either end of the piano to hit the dark bass notes as well as the high-pitched treble notes. I practiced stretching my small hands across eight keys to make an octave, always falling a little short. Although later I took piano lessons, there was a wonderful purity to the days when I simply stood in front of the piano exploring all the sounds I could make. The resonance of the notes and the excitement and curiosity with which I was able to play left a powerful impression.

As a therapist, I often use the analogy of playing all 88 keys on the piano when talking about experiencing the full range of our emotional life. At times, it may feel as though our lives are confined to just one or two octaves. We are inclined to repeat old notes and play familiar tunes. There may be a certain predictability and comfort to all this, but then we lose the beauty, range, and complexity that other sounds contribute. As I age, I find that there are still notes to be discovered. I could not have known the full range of grief, joy, and mystery that obtains as one grows older.

The trick in all this is to explore the basement, to look into dark and musty corners and allow ourselves and our clients to move out of familiar territory; then we can create new sounds and alliances and stretch for the octave. These are not always comfortable places, but dare I say, we will make more beautiful music.

— PART THREE —

Psychotherapist as Trickster — or, Crazy Like a March Hare

The Sacrifice of the Hare
and the Healing Dream

Holding the Seat

LOL

Meeting the Gypsy

This Way or That Way?

The Sacrifice of the Hare and the Healing Dream

As therapists, perhaps the greatest tricks are the ones we play on ourselves. We would not deliberately jump into the fire — but once there, along with our clients, we find capacities and possibilities of which we were previously unaware.

Many years ago, a wonderful book fell into my hands, *The Lady of the Hare: A Study in the Healing Power of Dreams*, by John Layard.[57] The book belonged to my mother-in-law, Sigrid McPherson, a Jungian analyst. When she died, I was given the gift of choosing some books from her collection, and this one stood out among all the rest. On its cover is a square botanical print in shades of green and gray. In its center are three hares running clockwise around an inverted triangle. I had never seen this image before; and yet I knew, immediately and instinctively, that it had meaning for me. It struck a deeply feminine chord. Over the thirty years that I have owned the book, I have returned to it many times, each time drawn into it more deeply and with increasing fascination.

I have chosen to share this experience with you because I want to describe how the inner life of the therapist so deeply and profoundly affects the work that she does with her clients as well as herself. There is an alchemical, transformative process when two people work closely together in therapy. How could it be otherwise? We affect one another and we change each other. *The Lady of the Hare* is a detailed account of an analytical process based upon the dreams of Mrs. Wright, a client of Dr. John Layard. What is most unusual is the effect of her dreams not only upon *her* unfolding awareness but upon *his* as well. When I first encountered the book, I was a young psychology student, fascinated by Layard's openness and willingness to deeply engage with his patient's material in both a personal and archetypal manner.

Mrs. Wright relates a series of dreams in which she feels that she must kill a hare, even though, she explains, "this seemed a terrible thing to do, but I had to do it."[58] In her dream she takes a kitchen knife and brings it down, cleaving the hare in two. As she kills the hare, she is taken with the odd appearance of satisfaction in its eyes. She has the distinct feeling that the creature is willing to lose its life on her behalf. As I pondered her dream, I could feel both the power and disgust of plunging the knife into the rabbit. This action, which would be unthinkable in waking life, could be accomplished symbolically through the dream.

What was the psychological meaning and purpose of her action? By taking the knife and bringing it down decisively through the rabbit, Mrs. Wright was able to break apart something solid in herself that needed to change. The feminine rabbit — or hare, in this case — symbolizes Mrs. Wright's sensitive and easily intimidated demeanor. In addition, the hare possesses a trickster quality that is integral to Mrs. Wright's awakening. Edward Edinger, in *Anatomy of the Psyche*, suggests, "psychologically, the result of separation by division into two is awareness of the opposites. This is a crucial feature of emerging awareness."[59] This explanation certainly seemed to be part of her dream process. Even more intriguing, however, was the fact that the hare welcomed its intended demise in the process. It watched compassionately while Mrs. Wright made this fearless gesture.

The Sacrifice of the Hare and the Healing Dream

In Mrs. Wright's conversations with Dr. Layard, the motivation for her action unfolded. By cleaving the hare in two, she was able to differentiate and perceive the forces of darkness and light in her personality. Her previous tendency to interpret all behavior as good and "for the best" had barred her from being in touch with her true feelings and experience of reality. She remained unaware of aspects of herself that resided in Shadow. This separation left her split off from her own deeper feelings and wisdom. Meanwhile, the hare's symbolic sacrifice, allowed the possibility of transformation for Mrs. Wright. Her psychological work lay in acknowledging previously unseen feelings and instincts that had been hidden by socialization and fear. In the last half of the book, Dr. Layard detailed many myths about the hare's capacity to sacrifice itself "by leaping into the fire and so transmuting his fleshly instinct into spirit, and its immediate connection to the moon, that 'light in the darkness' which illuminates the inner life of man."[60] He, too, was fascinated by the power of the dream and its archetypal significance.

I realized that my own psychological tendencies were caught up in a dilemma similar to Mrs. Wright's, hence my preoccupation and fascination with the book. I considered that perhaps the soft and vulnerable nature of Mrs. Wright made the hare an apt symbol for her predicament. Most curiously, I have always been fascinated by rabbits. I identify with the small, agile creature, and have kept several play rabbits of one kind or another in my office. Even now there is a small, white, leaping rabbit on my windowsill as well as a toy rabbit dressed in a black-and-white tuxedo that sits among my other stuffed animals. The tension of the opposites could not be more explicit and engaging than in his regal costume.

Dr. Layard made a point of differentiating the rabbit, which is common to North America, from the hare that is found in other parts of the world. In America, the Easter bunny, with which we are all familiar, derives from the European hare and its fertility. It has become a symbol of spring and new life. In Europe, the symbolic meaning of the hare is very ancient and more complex, being found commonly in Greece and Egypt. The hare and the moon coincide in festivals ushering in spring.

As I continued to plumb the meaning of Mrs. Wright's dream, the symbolic nature of the knife intrigued me. For many women, the knife is primarily a domestic implement used in the preparation of food. However, in the dream it clearly was a powerful tool of discernment. Wielding a sword or knife is a symbol of power and clarity of intention. When a woman needs to make important distinctions — to say "yes" to this, and "no" to that — she must distinguish between what she thinks and what she feels, what she needs for herself and how that affects the needs of others. When it is essential to make a choice on *her own behalf*, she must wield the sword with certainty and power, and not be confused and overly concerned by its impact on others. How difficult it can be to bring down the knife!

Dr. Layard and Mrs. Wright came to an understanding of her dreams through a process of discussion, talking at length about ideas and philosophy in a Socratic manner. The value of this kind of dialogue is frequently lacking in our current psychological methodology. We tend to undervalue ideas per se and their effect upon us. Layard often asked his client questions, to which she responded honestly and with curiosity. They discussed religion and belief and its place in life, a question that had also occupied Jung. I cringed, at times, feeling that Layard might be overly persuasive, particularly in regards to his own religious convictions. Nonetheless, the result of their powerful work together felt otherwise. He described their process in this way:

> We talked about the duality of everything: heaven and hell — darkness and light — day and night — good and evil — each pair composed of opposites necessary and complementary to one another…. I pointed out, and she finally agreed, that evil was necessary (i.e., inevitable) as well as good, so that anyone who tries to do good all the time, *must* fail because the other side has not been allowed for.[61]

Layard's discussions with Mrs. Wright about darkness and light were pivotal to her being able to move away from a one-sided perspective of her life, where she was identified with the light to the exclusion of the darkness. She was, it seemed, too good and too nice for her own benefit. She identified with the all-giving mother, kind and compassionate — wonderful traits, yet unbalanced and unrealistic. She was a devout Catholic who grew up in England in the 1920s. Like many women, she was raised to embody qualities of "goodness," exclusively. Other aspects of the personality were denigrated and reserved for the realm of the wicked or unacceptable. Layard suggested that Mrs. Wright's dreams reflected a change in society where "Christianity had got 'old' and was now having to be reborn out of our dreams."[62]

About a year before I finished writing *The Moon, the Hare, and the Pearl*, I returned to *The Lady of the Hare*. I took it off the shelf. I had not looked at it for some time. Nonetheless, it took hold of me once again and I could not put it down. I appreciated all that Layard had written about intuition and its connection to the hare. I realized that each time I returned to his writing, I was going to a well of inspiration. Layard's research and understanding of intuition validated this exceedingly inchoate and mysterious way of apprehending the world that resonated so deeply with me.

In my own work as a therapist, I have come to depend on the agility of the trickster-hare, a fragile yet indestructible creature that shows up when I need him the most, and often at the last possible minute. Many times in a session I may be searching for a common thread or catalyst — and suddenly, just at the end, when nothing seems forthcoming, an answer appears like a rabbit out of a hat. Such is the nature of intuition; it arrives whole and complete, flinging itself into a situation like a mercurial hare!

Through Mrs. Wright's highly evocative dream sequence, Layard also recognized a deep spiritual process at work in his client and himself. As a result, he undertook extensive research on the metaphoric meaning of the hare and its archetypal significance. Historically, animals have been used as ritual sacrifices; but Layard discovered that the hare, in particular, is represented in mythology throughout the world as a trickster associated with sacrifice. The hare acts as an agent of change and transformation, bringing pearls of wisdom to consciousness.

Meanwhile, the image on the cover of Layard's book, three hares running clockwise around an inverted triangle within a square, continued to fascinate me. It was embedded in my psyche. In 2016 my husband and I went to southern England to visit the ancient stones and feminine/goddess sites. One afternoon we visited Salisbury Cathedral, a very powerful and moving experience. (I would highly recommend it.) After several hours of walking the grounds and exploring the cathedral's magnificent interior, we went into the gift store and cafe that serves wonderful tea and scones. After buying gifts for my grandchildren and friends, I felt drawn to a shelf of books in the corner of the store. Just as many times before, one book stood out to me: *Stolen Images: Pagan Symbolism and Christianity*, by Peter Knight.[63] I immediately turned to the index and searched for hares, and there it was—the answer to the riddle was on pages 100-102! Here is his explanation:

> The Christian concept of the Holy Trinity is often expressed as three hares running in a circle, their three ears forming a triangle. He explains that this image has a long history, the earliest so far found being from China dated the 6th century.... It has been suggested that the triple hares signify the feminine aspect of divinity and fertility, connecting us back to the hare's association with the Moon, so long associated with goddesses. In the 17th century, during the persecution of women, hares became associated with witches and evil magic; *mad as a March hare* is still used today.

Peter Knight explained that in a small town near the cathedral, there were seventeen churches with images of hares! I am always thrilled and amazed at how intuition can be a driving force, how we know more than we understand or realize consciously in the moment, and, of course, how everything is connected like a chain of pearls. I often feel like my inner hare's nose is twitching, picking up a scent, hyper-alert to what is around me. I feel like an antenna!

My exploration of intuition and Layard's profound research and analysis is ongoing. I am planning a trip to Greece where, once again, I shall pursue the image of this fertile character, the fleet and complex hare. Symbolically, it possesses a compassionate spirit that permits it to enter the fire of transformation for the benefit of others. The hare as trickster is capable of sacrifice in service to something greater. As therapists, we might not deliberately jump into the psychological fire for ourselves; but once there with our clients, we may find capacities and possibilities of our own of which we were previously unaware. The brave hare lives deep in the psyche of us all.

Holding the Seat

Holding the seat means fully embodying the role of the therapist/healer/guide and not shying away from it. We become more at ease in liminal places, holding and acknowledging what we know and do not know.

It is 1:45 p.m., fifteen minutes before my client is to arrive. I go into my office, check the temperature, and adjust the heater. I sit down in my chair. I sense my body and how it knows this place. I notice what it is like to change from standing to sitting; and when I take my seat, this particular seat, I am aware of moving into my role that requires concentration, duty, and intention. I settle into my chair and experience a familiar sense of place. I take some deep breaths and meditate, letting go of thoughts and feelings I have brought with me. This brief period invites emptiness.

Before an actor takes the stage, there are physical exercises that she does to loosen up and make herself more malleable and available for her work. Ballet dancers do the same. They prepare the body and mind for the demands that will be made upon them. I have never heard of specific exercises like this for a psychotherapist, although I think they are certainly needed. Meanwhile, taking a few conscious breaths goes a long way.

My therapy office is across the driveway from my house. I often look out of my kitchen window and see my client sitting on a bench on the porch of my office. I might get some water or tea for us and then walk over to join them. We cross the threshold into the office together. The door closes and we move from a worldly environment into one that is quiet and private where we can expect no intrusions. We each take our respective seats. There is often a pause before either of us begins to speak. Now, before I sound too holy, I have to say there are times where the beginning of a session is more like a fashion show or weather report. Sometimes my client and I are wearing almost the same thing. (I find this a common synchronicity!) We talk about colors and shoes and whatever else seems pertinent. Sometimes we have to comment on pouring-down rain or blustery wind. Then we settle in and await the shift and the silence.

Holding the seat has both a literal and metaphoric meaning. In a literal sense, I have a very comfortable chair that I use when I work. It provides good support for my back and moves around easily on wheels. It allows me to move in closely to our conversation when needed, and to move back for a different view or perspective. When I am in my chair, I feel comfortable and relaxed. This is very important. We work with both body and mind. If we are out of sorts physically, we will be out of sorts mentally as well.

Many therapists, particularly those working in agencies, do not have a chair of their own and have to adapt to different arrangements in different rooms. This can be very challenging; when possible, bring your own chair! Remember, therapists work with their bodies, so take care of yours! Bring snacks and a good lunch. Stretch if you can between clients, and get a breath of fresh air. Go outside if it is a nice day. If there is a trick in any of this, it is the basics of showing up with an empty mind and a full belly.

Holding the seat also means fully embodying the role of therapist, guide, and expert. As you can imagine, this is a process born of experience. The therapist meets herself over and over again, watching her actions and responses, honing her skills. The ability to hold the seat accrues and matures over time. As you sit with your clients and work through challenges, you will develop your own techniques of questioning and discernment and you will become increasingly comfortable. You will feel confident sharing your observations with kindness and compassion. You will also be able to address moments in your conversation when you are not clear, when you feel that you have lost the thread. Then you can ask for clarification. When I work, I bring all that has accrued in me over the years. This allows me to be more open and at ease in liminal places, to trust the process and to love what I do. Holding the seat is one of the ideas that I discussed most with my interns.

When I prepare to work, I often feel as though I am putting on a special robe, an invisible costume that reminds me of my obligation and my service. As I dress to come to work, the costuming begins. (I know this because my husband usually announces my arrival in the living room, saying "Here's Dr. Gold.") I often wear a necklace that has meaning for me. For example, I wore a small, silver angel for all the years that I worked with abused children. I knew that the children could see her when they were looking at me. I also felt her support and guidance close to my heart.

In Zen practice, we speak about showing up for each moment, being present to whatever arises and not avoiding what is difficult and painful. Bringing this awareness to therapy is essential; it keeps us honest and open. This is an example of the kind of rootedness needed to hold the seat. I think of couples counseling, where there are often moments of discomfort and contentiousness. Working with couples takes a lot of skill and practice. It often requires that the therapist bring forth a voice that is firm and decisive. That does not mean that there isn't room for laughter, because there really is, especially with couples; but being able to be firm, cool, and declarative is also needed.

For example, I might decide to tell the couple that they will be using only "I" statements in the session, that there will be no "I feel that you..." statements. This usually requires some explanation, because I am asking them to resist a habitual pattern of blaming, and I have to hold them to it. When I gently and firmly bring each person back to owning his or her own feelings, arguing and blaming come to a grinding halt. Clients often laugh at their frustration. Sometimes they get pissed off and direct it at me but if I can help them to stick to it, they will be able to discover what is under their judgments and projections. Each person will be able to feel his/her *own* feelings — usually, grief, sadness, and disappointment. Then we have something to work with.

The more you work as a therapist, the more comfortable you will become holding the seat. You will feel rooted as you connect to yourself and your client, and take support from the earth as you sit in awareness. You will become more adept at the transition from your personal life and concerns into the space of the therapist/guide. Your intention will strengthen as your skills mature, and your seat will feel like home.

As a therapist, you learn to meet the moment with everything you've got, and with everything you can give. That's all there is — your humanity, your skill, your compassion, your honesty, and your soul.

LOL

Humor is the best trick of all. It is a great common denominator. Laughing at our selves is good medicine.

I have to tell you a funny story. Many years ago, my office was in my home in Santa Barbara. It was located at the end of the front hall, just past the kitchen. One day during a session, my client and I heard a very strange noise coming from the kitchen that sounded like running water. I went out to see what was going on. There, in the kitchen, was an avalanche of soapsuds all over the floor, glistening in the sunlight. Although the dishwasher was closed, it was still exploding with bubbles oozing around the edges! I called my client in to see the avalanche. Once I got over the shock, we laughed and laughed at the silliness of it all. I felt like I was in an episode of "I Love Lucy."[64] I had run out of dishwasher detergent and, without really thinking about it, I had put in dish soap instead. Who knew? What a great moment! I still treasure the memory.

Having an office in your home means that you, the therapist, have to accept more transparency than if you practiced in a professional building. There is no question that working from home is a more intimate situation. The client sees how and where you live, at least to some degree. You cannot help but take on more ordinary proportion, especially if the client needs to use your bathroom. I have to remind myself to put all my pills and vitamins away in the medicine chest as well as keep it clean and presentable. I have had fantasies about a client's reading my prescriptions and diagnosing me! The client now sees you, contextually, as a "normal" person.

How does this affect the transference? This is a difficult question, but I think we can safely assume that transference is inevitable. The client will see the therapist as some aspect of their parent or inner constellation, and even more, they will project various qualities upon them as needed psychologically. A typical therapy office (out of the home) ensures that the therapist-client encounter is very controlled and regulated — a paradigm that belongs to a medical model that enhances distance between patient and doctor. Sometimes this distance is absolutely needed for safety when working with certain individuals. Therefore, I usually meet clients for a ½ hour interview before deciding on whether or not I will take them in treatment. I also do a phone interview first as another screening method. There are many ways and contexts in which to work. *You must find what is comfortable for you.* Seeing the therapist in her home tells the client a lot about how you live and even what matters to you. I find this acceptable but you have to be prepared to be more visible and transparent and realize that the client will be affected by what he or she sees.

In my current workspace, my clients enter through the garden of my house, which is over 100 years old. They walk down a serpentine brick path and into an enclosed stone patio with old vines and trees. The doorway to my office is at the end of the patio and is quite private. Sometimes, people come a little early and are welcome to sit outside and enjoy the garden. The boundaries are a little blurred and the lines of demarcation not so crisp. I feel fortunate to be able to work in this way.

I have to confess one more incident in service to humor and the perils of a home office. Several years ago, my office was in a little cottage across the driveway from my house. I could see people from my kitchen window sitting on the porch waiting for me, and that was always a good visual cue. However, one morning at 9:30, I heard the doorbell ring at my house, not at the cottage. Although I was still in my bathrobe, I felt compelled to answer the door. Before my eyes were two elderly people, a husband and wife, who were new clients. Holy shit! I had forgotten their appointment. What could I say? I apologized profusely, of course, and thought I would never see them again. (I told this story to my interns who imagined that I do everything perfectly. That is so not true.) The amazing thing is that this wonderful couple came to therapy for quite some time and we shared a rich and enlivening conversation together.

So what does this tell us? First, we can never really know what will matter to another person or how a particular word or gesture or smile will touch them. The alchemy of relationship is subtle and complex; we can only be truthful and as real as we can be. It also reminds me that laughter is the other side of sorrow, as comedy is the other side of tragedy. These are inextricable pairs that cannot be separated. I often laugh at myself and I am way past pretending that I get it all right or "have it all together." The archetype of the Fool is a valuable teacher for me. After all, foolishness is the other side of wisdom!

Moments when the client and I meet in humor are priceless. Laughter is a common denominator that cuts through the one-up position of the therapist. Therapy is not always serious, nor should it be. I have a cartoon on my desk of a therapist, probably a psychoanalyst, who is sitting behind her client, who is lying on the couch. The client is a large egg wearing striped socks — Humpty-Dumpty, I presume. The caption reads: "Eventually I'd like to see you able to put yourself back together!" This aspiration tickles me and Lord knows, it applies to me as well.

Meeting the Gypsy

Sometimes I receive a call from a prospective client and I am aware that my inner gypsy is listening in. She is playful, insightful, and occasionally capricious. She sees beyond what I could rationally know.

When I was in graduate school, my professor asked the class if we had an image of ourselves as a psychotherapist. Instantly, before my eyes, was a gypsy, sitting at a table gazing into a crystal ball. I recognized her immediately as a familiar companion and inner figure. The gypsy lives on the outskirts of town. She is an outlier and not part of the collective. She stays with her own tribe. Her nature is mercurial and not easily deciphered. The gypsy receives impressions from other realms. She looks beyond the literal to see more clearly what the future holds.

"Went to See the Gypsy" was a song written by Bob Dylan in 1970.[65] This song begins with a seeker looking for guidance. Although the gypsy is available, the seeker hesitates. He is distracted and leaves to make a phone call. A dancing girl, perhaps an inner anima figure, encourages him to return, but he procrastinates. In these precious moments, he misses an opportunity. When he returns, the gypsy is gone. There are synchronous moments in our lives when we have the opportunity to meet the gypsy, the wise woman or wise man, the therapist, the guru or the one "who knows." How we respond at that moment changes everything. Do we listen to our intuition or do we ignore it?

Several months ago, I had my own meeting with a seer. My husband and I had gone to see our dentist, who lives in the ocean-side town of Bolinas near San Francisco. While my husband was getting his teeth cleaned, I wandered outside. Sitting on the sidewalk by the park was a young man perhaps in his thirties. In front of him was a hand-written sign that read "Palm Reader." I had noticed him on the way into the office and felt myself hesitate to approach him, even though I was intrigued. Now I walked toward him to take a closer look. In front of him on the ground was a piece of purple velvet, and on it were stones, crystals, and several tarot cards. His fingernails were dirty, his clothes tattered, and he looked like he had been on the road. His eyes smiled. "Would you like a reading?" he asked simply. "Yes," I replied, as I sat down on the sidewalk. So it began.

He asked if I had any particular questions or concerns. I said that I did not and that a general sense of my future would do. He took my hand, held it, and was silent. He studied my palm as though words and ideas were spelled out in every crevice. Then he began to speak in a soft, clear voice with a lilting cadence, telling me what he observed and intuited. I had never had my palm read in such detail or with such delicacy.

The reading from the sidewalk gypsy was profound, as was its effect upon me. I realized that in order to receive what he had to offer, I had to let go of my preconceived ideas and doubts about him so that I could listen. In the same way, the gypsy therapist shares with her client what she intuits. Then it is up to the client to suspend judgment long enough to consider what is being offered.

So, my dear fellow gypsies, as an experiment, you may want to close your eyes, relax and, if you have not done so already, hold the question: "Who am I when I am in the role of the therapist?" Take your time and write freely about whatever comes to you. Let your imagination have free reign.

Meeting the Gypsy

You may discover some rich inner voices and resources that accompany you when you work. Lastly, do not take this all too seriously; you already know the answer!

Skillful Means

When a session feels dry or unproductive, the therapist is faced with a choice. She can continue with things as they are, or she can instigate a shift. The trick is to change directions gracefully. Trust yourself, trust your client, and be mindful of which way the wind is blowing.

As therapists, we make many subtle choices in the course of the therapeutic dialogue. Sometimes we push, sometimes we wait; we challenge or we defer. When I am at a choice point, I often feel as though I am putting my hands up in the air to test the wind. Which way is it blowing? Do I go with the wind, or tack and take a new direction? As an intuitive-feeling type, I cannot tell you exactly how I decide; but I can say that I am moved at times by the trickster archetype, the unconventional wisdom. I am not talking about being capricious for no reason. I am talking about being "crazy like a March hare."

Knowing when to change direction and to shift the energy in a session requires knowing how the process between you and the client feels. Is it flowing or is it dry? Is it lacking something vital? When the verbal process feels non-productive or as though you have come to a natural stopping point, consider taking another route. Sometimes shifting direction can occur when you notice a breadcrumb on the path that you had not seen before. It has a little sparkle to it and feels numinous. You choose to pick it up. The unconscious is always in play, like a river running under the conversation between you and your client.

Some time ago, I had just such an experience in a session. My client Susan, a young woman in her twenties, came in quite upset about a sudden ending to her romantic relationship. She recounted how her boyfriend had lied to her about his feelings for her and had been seeing someone else at the same time. In response, when she learned about this betrayal, she ended the relationship but still had doubts about herself and her naiveté. She was angry with him but also blamed herself. Why had she not seen this deception coming? "Why did I not know?" she lamented. "Why was I so stupid?" she asked.

It was clear that Susan blamed herself. What she referred to as her "stupidity" was really her trusting attitude and innocence. She had been fooled, as many women have, by the guile of Bluebeard, a compelling, convincing, and charming persona that masks an untrustworthy interior. We talked for some time about Susan's misplaced feelings of guilt and shame, but this did little to soothe her. She sat back in her chair, exhausted. I, too, sat back and took a deep breath. We were silent. I waited. Then an idea came to me like a hare leaping before me. "How would you like to hear a story, a fairy tale?" I asked her. There was another moment of silence. Then I saw her eyes get bigger as she entertained the idea. "Yes," she said with a smile. "Great," I replied.

My story began, as all fairy tales do, with "Once upon a time...." What a wonderful invitation to allow ourselves to fall into the world of our imagination. As I regaled her with the story of *Bluebeard*, we both became entranced. *Bluebeard* is a powerful tale about the innocence of the young feminine and her almost inevitable encounter with the devouring masculine. Love is blind, especially young love, and it is a condition that always portends danger. It is easy to be blind-sided by someone whose motive is different from what you had imagined and different from your own, I told her.

> In this old fairytale, a very dashing stranger who had recently come to town approached three sisters. "Could I take you for a ride on the lake?" he asked them. This was a very exciting offer and the three sisters happily agreed. After their excursion, they could not wait to go home and talk about their experience. The older two sisters acknowledged that the stranger was, indeed, very handsome and interesting and funny; but, then, had anyone noticed that his beard seemed a little blue? The middle sister said she, too, had noticed a strange cast to his beard. But the youngest and most naive said, "Absolutely not. He is so handsome and charming. How can you say such things?"

> The following day, the stranger came knocking at the door of their cottage once again. "Would you like to join me for a picnic?" he asked the sisters in oily tones. Once again, they all agreed and did, in fact, have a lovely time. He played the flute, charming them with music and song. Nonetheless, after this encounter, the two older sisters were even more convinced that there was something very odd, even untrustworthy, about this fellow whose beard was a very unusual blue!

> "How easy it is to be fooled," thought the oldest sister. She tried to warn her youngest sister but she would have none of it. The very next day the stranger knocked once again at the door of the tiny cottage. This was their third encounter.

[The number three in fairy tales often predicts a shift or change in consciousness.]

> The stranger now asked for the hand of the youngest sister in marriage, and she readily agreed. Of course, the

wedding took place immediately, before anyone could give it a second thought. After the wedding, the stranger and his young bride left the little village and went straight to his castle on the edge of the forest. Everything went along rather smoothly for the young bride until her husband announced that he was leaving on a business trip. Before leaving, he brought her a large set of keys on a golden ring. "You may use all of these keys," he said, "except for this one tiny key that belongs to a room in the cellar. Do not use this key under any circumstances," he said in threatening tones.

"I won't, I won't," she promised. Then he left.

Eventually, the youngest sister became lonely while her husband was gone. She called her sisters to come for a visit. When they arrived, they wandered happily around the castle trying out the keys and opening all the doors to the rooms, until they came to the tiny door in the basement. "Open it," the sisters implored her. "No," she said. "I must not." Now the shoe was on the other foot. The older sisters, perhaps unconsciously, knew that the door ought to be opened so that the secret could be exposed.

"No, no," the youngest persisted, but her curiosity was too much! She took the key and opened it tentatively. Immediately she saw skeletons upon skeletons with remnants of bridal clothes wrapped around their bones. She slammed the door shut and put the key in the pocket of her dress. As she did so, the key dripped blood down her white apron. "Oh, what shall I do, what shall I do?" she cried. She tried hiding the key in her dresser drawer but the secret was out. The sisters, after causing much havoc, went home, leaving her to her fate.

A few days later, the youngest daughter's husband returned to the castle. Immediately, he asked her for the keys and when she surrendered them reluctantly, he saw that the tiniest key was missing. He knew that she had opened the forbidden door. "You have disobeyed me," he growled. "Now you, too, must die." The young wife asked only that she be allowed to go up into the tower to pray before her death. He granted her this last wish. While in the tower, she sent a signal to her sisters and brothers, who came to her rescue immediately. We do not know exactly how she did this, but in three shakes of a lamb's tail, they arrived and did away with the treacherous Bluebeard! The sisters were reunited, peace returned to the tiny village, and all was well.

The story felt thick around us. It had worked its magic. Susan laughed a little and sighed. She appeared relaxed when she left the session.

The power of the tale carried our work along in a beautiful, metaphoric way. Mythic stories offer tremendous depth and do so in a way that can be taken in and absorbed over time. Shifting energy through the story allowed Susan to move away from her self-recrimination. Instead, she could concentrate on bringing her own resources to the fore. Over time, Susan saw through the veil of her innocence and was able to energize her inner wise woman. As a result, she could unmask the inner predator. In *Women Who Run with the Wolves*,[66] Clarissa Pinkola Estes writes:

> Developing a relationship with the wildish nature is an essential part of women's individuation. In order to execute this, a woman must go into the dark, but at the same time she must not be irreparably trapped, captured, or killed on her way there or back.[67]

In my experience as a supervisor, I have noticed that for a new therapist, shifting directions in a session can feel like the first time you drove a stick shift on a hill and thought you might slide back down helplessly. How do you use the brake and the gas at the same time? Does stopping the action suggest to the client that whatever was happening was somehow wrong or not good enough? When the shift is mindful, you will know what to do. If the client does not want to transition into something else, they will tell you or keep talking. To continue the car metaphor, you are shifting gears because that will allow you to drive more smoothly and efficiently. Initiating a pause, a moment of mindfulness, can create an opportunity for clarity and vitality. So sit back in your chair, change your posture, and check in with your body. Perhaps move the chair back a bit, allowing for more space between you and your client. This simple adjustment allows your gaze to soften. Then wait for inspiration and intuition to guide both you and your client. Trust the process and allow the silence to happen.

Another possibility for shifting energy in a session is asking your client if they would like to do a sand tray. If the client agrees, she will leave her chair and move toward the shelves and the sand tray figures. This simple act changes the dynamic in the room. Your client is now moving and actively engaged in perusing the shelves in search of something that speaks to her *in the moment*. When this happens, I shift my position so that I can watch her process. I am also now engaged in a different way. I am supporting her through my attention, but without speaking. As she creates the tray, she brings aliveness to her process.

The power of this intervention was very palpable for Linda, a middle-aged woman who came into treatment describing her concern as "apathy." She felt that she was often lethargic and lacking in motivation. She was unable to do her creative work or, at times, even clean the house. She procrastinated and then felt annoyed with herself. She could not understand her resistance. She felt stymied by her inner battle and hoped to find some resolution.

Prior to our first session, I had the opportunity to observe her walking through the garden toward my office. I was struck by her elegance. Tall and lanky, she had an unusual gait. Her strides were long and measured. She appeared to be meditating as she walked. At the same time, an image flitted through my mind of a praying mantis. "How odd," I thought, "this juxtaposition" — which, as it turned out, presaged the nature of her inner struggle. I filed it away.

In our first session, she offered history related to her frustration with herself that included issues with work and relationship. We were near the end of the session when I noticed that she had turned slightly toward the sand tray shelves. When I saw this gesture, I had a moment of choice. I could wait until the next session to offer the use of the tray, or I could pay attention to what was happening with her in the moment. Although it was close to the end of the session, I wanted to seize the moment. I asked if she was interested in the sand tray and whether or not she was familiar with it. She had used it once before, she said. "Would you like to use the sand tray today?" I asked. Her eyes lit up. "Yes," she said, rather emphatically. She explained that she had been curious about the figures on the shelves and what they might mean; one had already been calling to her.

Linda stood up, took a basket, and began choosing different miniatures with apparent ease. She asked if there was a limit to how many she could take. I assured her that there was not, she could have as many as she liked. She smiled delightedly. Linda began by creating a room with a rocking chair, a dog, and a miniature easel. She spoke a little as she worked, humming to herself. I noticed that her feeling of apathy seemed dispelled. When she was finished, she appeared quite satisfied with her effort. We both stood quietly in front of the tray and appreciated what she had made.

This was the first of Linda's sand tray explorations. Working in the sand had ignited her creativity and expressiveness. The apathy that she had initially described seemed to melt away when the artist in her had a chance to play. Working in the sand became vital to her process. As she continued to use the tray, she brought in images of anger and resentment toward herself and a previous relationship. It was then that I recalled my momentary impression of a praying mantis that had been lurking under her controlled exterior. I was glad that I had caught the little glimmer in her eye and the curiosity in her gesture, as she turned toward the shelves in her first session. Her instinct and intuition about her own healing had moved our process forward.

Some of you are already doing somatic work, art therapy, or drama therapy with your clients, and you have learned techniques for changing directions and modalities in a session as well as methods for inviting in the client's playful self. These modalities are very useful in moving from passive to active mode and into a more embodied and vital experience. Weaving in a different technique in a session uses skillful means to bring aliveness and immediacy into the conversation and the present moment. Trust yourself and your client when changing direction. If it is not a good idea, the client will let you know. Be mindful of the way the wind is blowing; then, whatever happens, you are likely to wind up somewhere you need to go.

— PART FOUR —

On the Practice of Suffering and Joy

Theater and Therapy

Psychotherapy as Confession

Kindness Toward the Self

In the Beginning Is the Ending

Resist Contrivance

Last Thoughts

Theater and Therapy

"An actor must work all his life, cultivate his mind, train his talents systematically, develop his character: he may never despair and never relinquish this main purpose — to love the art with all his strength and love it unselfishly."
— Constantin Stanislavski

For those therapists for whom their work is their art, Stanislavski's dictum applies. A therapist, like an actor, must develop her character. The word *character* comes from the Greek, meaning "to engrave; the aggregate of particular qualities that constitute individuality or identity."[68] This definition evokes the image of a face deeply lined with emotion, expression, and many experiences of life. As a therapist, all that we have felt, heard, and encountered in the course of our life becomes grist for the mill of our professional work as well as a storehouse from which we can draw.

Stanislavski describes a parallel process in the development of an actor. He suggests that the actor complete an analysis of his role. In doing so, the actor must bring all of his experience and knowledge of himself and his training to the fore. Stanislavsky's use of the word "analysis" most probably derives from his knowledge of *psycho*analysis. He writes:

> What is the point of departure for an analysis? Let us make use of the one-tenth part of ourselves which in art as in life is attributed to the mind, so that with its aid we can appeal to the work of our feelings, and after that, when our feelings reach the point of expression, let us try to understand their direction and unobtrusively guide them along the true creative path. In other words, let our unconscious,

intuitive creativeness be set in motion by the help of the conscious preparatory work. Through the conscious to the unconscious — that is the motto of our art and technique.[69]

The work of both therapist and actor takes study, preparation, and years of practice. Theater and therapy inform each other. Both emanate from the same source, the desire to understand and express the human drama. The Greek plays of Aeschylus, Euripides, and Sophocles contributed to our initial understanding of human behavior. These playwrights plumbed the depth of human emotions through the genres of tragedy and comedy. They explored the full range of life experience: joy and despair, gain and loss, love and hatred, greed and benevolence. Unfortunately, we rarely study these mythic plays as part of the preparation for our work as psychotherapists. Shakespeare's plays continued in the rich tradition of elucidating our behavior, cautioning us against our excesses and validating our passions. *Macbeth*, *Romeo and Juliet*, and *Hamlet* are now integral to our modern psyche.

Early in my career as a therapist, I noticed my own propensity for theater. I realized that sometimes my manner changed in response to my client's presentation. I sensed that my instinctive adaptation was based on the interplay of opposites: anima/animus (feminine/masculine), mother/father, wise/foolish, open/avoidant, etc. I wondered whether my manner was an unconscious suggestion to the client's psyche as I played out the other side of the pair. My mutability informed me as to my own countertransference. What part in the client's drama did I play? Who were they in mine, I asked myself?

As a therapist, I find myself taking on different roles. One of my favorites is the Jewish Mother who speaks with a

Brooklyn accent. She is an outgrowth of my intuitive self who is self-assured. Of course, she's right! Of course, she knows what to do! She is full of opinions and in any moment may offer one of them. I must confess that she is so much a part of my panoply of selves that I almost left her out of the book — and now, towards the end, I realize my omission. Like the 13th fairy in *Sleeping Beauty*, one must never forget to invite her to the table! I use her like a tincture, in concentrated doses. She certainly has her uses.

Like theater, therapy reveals a person's character and story. Both therapist and client arrive on stage in costume; we take our designated seats and play out the scene. When the actors or selves are present and accounted for, the client investigates his or her motives and actions and makes decisions as to how the plot will unfold. Early in my studies, I read the work of Sheldon Kopp, a brilliant and very funny psychiatrist who wrote *This Side of Tragedy: Psychotherapy as Theater*.[70] Kopp was wonderfully authentic, funny, and irreverent. He wrote:

> Too often, as children, we are encouraged to try to be something other than ourselves. It is demanded that we assume a character not our own, live out a life story written by another. The plot line is given. Improvisations are unacceptable, and the direction is a form of close-quarter tyranny. Neurosis is in part the result of being miscast into a scenario plotted out in accord with somebody else's unfulfilled dreams and unfaced anxieties.[71]

Of course, Kopp was describing his own derailment in his family, and his difficult and challenging struggle to find his true self as he reached maturity. I can think back on many clients who have assured me that they must have been born into the wrong family! They never felt that they belonged and they could not imagine how it had happened! They were the black sheep, the misunderstood and blamed children who could find no meaning in their suffering and no redemption. I imagine that, like many therapists, I have always had a soft spot in my heart for the black sheep, the outsider, and the lost child.

Robert was just such a man. He was an engineer, a thinking type, and serious in his presentation. Initially, I spoke in his language as a basis for trust and comfort. I drew on all of the engineering metaphors and language I possessed. Later, I shifted to more emotional and playful responses that elicited different kinds of reactions from him. Robert was used to playing a particular part in life, a diligent and responsible man, serious; and yet I sensed much more to him. Perhaps there was playfulness behind his eyes and a dry humor in his responses.

He was in a new relationship and he was having difficulty communicating with his partner. It was hard for him to understand her expression of emotion, and even more difficult to generate and express his own. He did, in fact, feel things deeply, but they remained inchoate, and hard to grasp. Sometimes I would gently chide and encourage him to let go "just a little." Then he would laugh and become more aware of his stock responses. Our sessions entailed a gentle practice of coming into contact with his feelings in both mind and body. When he stepped out of his professional role, his emotions became more accessible to him.

I suggested that he might enjoy using the sand tray. He met the suggestion enthusiastically. He found some figures that reminded him of his childhood: the Smurfs, with their goofy hair; some Lincoln logs; and toy soldiers. A flash of delight appeared on his face as he gathered the figures. "Let yourself play," I advised. "Let your imagination create whatever it wishes."

Working in the sand became an opening into a younger self who had been more in touch with his feelings. His domineering father, an engineer who was strict and exacting, had strongly influenced his character. His father had often become impatient with his mother, a more emotionally expressive person. Like Sheldon Kopp, Robert had been miscast into a role that did not suit him. Nonetheless, by becoming emotionally unavailable and quiet, he had found a way to survive his early years. His persona belied a more diverse and complex character.

I asked Robert if he recalled a younger, more tender aspect of himself. He recalled chasing butterflies in nearby fields and taking long walks at the beach when he was a child. He said that he had been quite content when engaged in nature. Using the sand tray created a safe place for him to rediscover these tendencies.

Dora Kalff[72] described the sand tray as a free and protected space, a *temenos*.[73] Within its boundaries, a person can safely express whatever is needed. In many ways I find that the tray functions like a small theater or stage, capable of holding rich emotion and expression as well as unconscious material through the use of figures arranged by the client. There is, of course, no script. Rather, the client responds to her own internal process, choosing characters and scenery that reflect both conscious and unconscious meaning. As Robert continued to work in the sand, he touched into tender parts of himself as well as his own "inner living spirit." He was able to embody more fully all the gifts of his character.

The wonder of therapy as theater is that it makes room on the psychological stage for all of our hidden figures, those aspects of us that have remained behind the scenes often exerting their influence unconsciously. These are our miscast villains, our Shadow, whose presence is needed in service to transformation. It also invites in the lovers and the angels, all the players who hide in the corners of psyche, and asks them to come out and speak. Embracing our full cast of characters, we realize that we are both villain and angel alike. Then the deep work of healing and accepting the full self with compassion begins. We come to understand that we all suffer each in her own way, and that no one is truly isolated in her role. As Shakespeare said in *As You Like It*: "All the world's a stage, and all the men and women merely players," and so it is.

Psychotherapy as Confession

Our work as a therapist is wrapped in privilege. Like a confession, it lives sequestered in each of us in a vault of silence. We carry the burden willingly, but like our clients, we need to surrender it and offer it up to the gods.

We sat across from each other for the first time. He was a young man in his thirties, casually dressed, with intense blue eyes. He twisted slightly in his seat. "I have never told anyone this before," he began. I took a breath, inhaling slowly, sensing what was about to be revealed. This was not the first time that a client's revelations had come so quickly with no preamble, as if fate had contrived this moment of confession. He continued, haltingly at times, while intermittently words and sounds poured from his throat. His eyes looked far away, as if searching the past for long-held images, unspeakable moments of fear and grief. As a young boy he had been raped repeatedly by his uncle, he explained. The secret had been spoken, and now lay shimmering and tender between us.

He stopped speaking. Everything in me slowed down to make space to hold his words and feelings. I breathed deeply. I could feel my face changing, my eyes softening, searching his expression, to meet him. My hand moved instinctively to my heart. "I am so sorry," I said. "I am so sorry." He choked and sputtered as tears washed over his face. Then we both waited in silence, allowing a deep feeling of relief to sink in. He had made his confession.

As a therapist, you will find yourself in the position of receiving a confession many times over. You will bear witness to the grief and sorrow of another person, and you will feel the intimate challenge of holding whatever has been revealed. To receive these intimate feelings and to bear witness to the suffering of another person is a privilege and, at times, a burden as well.

I first contemplated the meaning of confession when I read *Magister Ludi: The Glass Bead Game*, by Hermann Hesse.[74] This book may also have been the first pearl in my conscious understanding that everything is connected, no matter how unlikely and distant things may appear to be. In the appendix to *The Glass Bead Game* is a short story called "Father Confessor."[75] It is the story of Josephus Famulus, a young hermit who lives an ascetic life in the mountains. Despite his intended solitude, people come from great distances to confess to him because they have heard that he is kind, non-judgmental, and fully accepting of all that is brought to him. He possesses the gift of listening, and he performs this service willingly and freely for many years. Hesse describes him in this way:

> He seemed to pass no judgment upon them and to feel neither pity nor contempt for the person confessing. His function was to arouse confidence and to be receptive, to listen patiently and lovingly, helping the imperfectly formed confession to take shape, inviting all that was dammed up or encrusted within each soul to flow and pour out. When it did, he received it and wrapped it in silence.[76]

This beautiful and poetic description reminds me of our highest calling in psychotherapy: to listen without judgment, to accept all that comes, and to create a space for healing. We are not always without judgment, nor are we in the business of absolution; but we function in the tradition of the good and wise parent who listens with compassion and kindness.

Psychotherapy as Confession

Hesse suggests that the function of a confessor is to arouse confidence in the penitent so that he is able to go on with his life despite the burden he carries. The confession is "unformed dough" that is molded into a loaf, baked in the oven, and made digestible. This image reflects the alchemical nature of psychotherapy, in which unconscious material comes to awareness by being heated in the therapeutic vessel. Then it is consumed, digested, and made available to transformation.

After many years of service to others, Josephus finds that he, himself, feels disturbed and overwhelmed. Full of doubt and confusion, he can no longer listen to other people's stories and suffering. His own soul calls out to him, asking him to reflect on his *own* life. Confused and struggling, he leaves his hut and goes in search of someone to hear his confession. He has heard of another confessor, Father Dion, who is also a hermit. Father Dion's manner is quite different from his own. He is a wise counselor of souls, a great judge, a chastiser, and rectifier. His approach to absolution is quite different from that of Josephus. He is stern and harsh; but, in the end, the results are the same: the sinner leaves feeling absolved and able to go on with his life.

The remainder of Hesse's story describes the unfolding relationship between these two men. Both have received many confessions. Ironically, they meet at a time when each has the need to unburden himself to the other. They have been filled up by the sorrows and errors of others, as well as having accrued their own distress and confusion. Both are in need of spiritual sustenance, confession, forgiveness, and renewal. Over a period of many years, the men learn to serve one another so that both can find peace of mind.

The story "Father Confessor" is important for therapists who will most certainly, at times, find themselves overwhelmed or burned out. There was a time in my own career when I had to take three months off work because I was so sad. I cried at the drop of a hat. I had been the supervisor of the sexual-abuse treatment team for some time. We met weekly, and every week a large pile of cases to distribute sat in front of me. In my work at an agency I treated sexually abused children, and in my own private practice I saw many sexually abused adults. I felt like there was no end to it. Was everybody abused? Was the world a terribly dangerous place? I needed to stop, rest, and recover my sense of proportion. I had to grieve, and also to laugh again. I needed to confess to others my vulnerability so that I could rest and heal.

Like Josephus, every therapist must find a way to unburden him or herself, whether through the compassionate listening of a friend, a partner, or their own therapist. Walking in nature, running, doing yoga, creating art, or practicing meditation are also helpful. When you work as a therapist, the need to process your own feelings and behavior is ongoing. How could it be otherwise? You, too, need a safe harbor where you can discuss all that is being stirred in you. Perhaps you will talk with a therapist or choose to be in a supervision group with your peers where you can speak freely about all of your concerns.

Do you recall the expression to *pour your heart out*? I hardly hear it used any more. It is a powerful image. To pour as if from a large pitcher, to spill over — this phrase has fallen away from common usage, probably because of its emotionality. It describes allowing the heart to empty, to liquefy so that it can release emotion and concern. I sense that emptying implies pouring your heart out *to* someone who can *receive* it, like the monk Josephus. In the act of pouring out your heart, you shed tears and are also watered by them. A similar process of letting go repeats in therapy. With all of a client's self-perceived shortcomings and concerns out on the table, the therapist receives them and says *yes* to it all; she receives the confession. Her acceptance is pivotal for the client, who is ultimately challenged to accept it as well.

There is a saying that "confession is good for the soul." The word *soul* has also been largely forgotten in much of psychology, although *psyche* is at the core of its very meaning. The seduction of science, of something practical, tangible, and verifiable, is easier to hold than something as diaphanous and elusive as soul. Nonetheless, I believe it is the soul's longing that initially brings the client into the consulting room in search of healing.

It is interesting to notice how language has shifted away from words like *cares, troubles*, and *soul*. The word *burden*, too, has gone out of daily usage. All of these descriptors have been replaced, at least in psychological parlance, with "issues." Everyone has issues! As is true with much of our current language, the new term is less soulful and sonorous. It carries no emotional valence, and we cannot locate it in our body. On the other hand, a burden evokes a very physical image, something that weighs us down and is carried on our shoulders or borne like a cross. Body-centered therapies instruct us in the value of body-mind integration. After all, the body remembers and the body speaks.

Emotion lives embodied in our whole being. We know that emotional receptors are located not only in the heart and brain but also in the gut, in all parts of us. We cannot be subdivided. When we ache with what we cannot control or accept, the body announces it through a symptom and manifests it until such time as we are willing or capable of embracing it and letting it go.

As therapists, we need to recognize how deeply we are moved by the work that we do. We listen daily to the pain of others and know that we cannot carry our clients' suffering alone, or we will be consumed. We need to take care of our own burdens and offer them up to the fire, to the gods. Making our own confession asks us to plumb the depths of our faith and understanding about human life and the nature of suffering and joy. In this way, psychotherapy is a spiritual practice that takes us to the farthest reaches of what we know and understand and asks us to explore and open ourselves to life in the deepest way we can.

Kindness Toward the Self

The trick is not to avoid or deny what is difficult in ourselves but to meet it with kindness and compassion, because that is our humanity.

Many years ago I saw a therapist shortly after my first marriage ended. I was thirty-six years old and very unhappy; but also, I was exceedingly critical of myself. The therapist insisted on telling me that there was nothing wrong with me, and that I had done nothing wrong! How could this possibly be true? He never faltered in his perception. I was unable to persuade him that I had *serious* flaws. He was kind and funny, intelligent and loving. I struggled with accepting myself, and allowing myself to be who I was. Over time, I softened, and a gentle humor toward myself was restored. I often think back on our time together and the deep lessons in self-acceptance I learned from him.

When I became a therapist and began working with my own clients, I noticed that they, too, were hard on themselves and unforgiving. I wondered what might encourage them to be kinder toward themselves and to take a more compassionate stance toward their perceived shortcomings. How does a person refrain from harsh judgment and the tendency to be self-critical? How can a person learn to be gentler, softer, and more compassionate toward the tender parts of themselves?

Zen practice urges us to stay present to our pain rather than hiding from it, because running away only prolongs its hold on us. This is not an easy thing to do. Avoidance, deflection, and distraction are virtually automatic behaviors that we have learned over our lifetime. Self-blame, guilt, and shame all rear their ugly heads with little provocation. One approach to minimize our suffering is through meditative awareness; we can learn to stay present to our thoughts and feelings in a gentle way, just noticing whatever happens. I often spend time with clients sitting and just noticing. We practice for 10 or 15 minutes, and I encourage them to continue at home. Most people find that this soothes them very quickly as they begin to make a space between their thoughts and sense of self. Mindfulness practice teaches us to observe without judgment. In this way we begin to bring gentleness and compassion toward the self. Staying present to whatever thoughts and feelings arise in us is a deep and courageous practice.

In working with clients around self-acceptance and compassion, I often turn to the work of Stephen Levine, particularly his book *Healing into Life and Death*.[77] This book offers many compassionate meditations for dealing with illness and suffering. I practice "A Simple Meditation" with my clients:

> Sitting comfortably, allow the attention to come gradually to the breath. The breath coming and going all by itself, deep within body. Take a few moments to allow the attention to gather within the even rhythm of the breath.
>
> Turning gently within, begin to direct toward yourself feelings of loving-kindness, relating to yourself as though you were your only child. Silently in the heart say,
>
> "May I dwell in the heart. May I be free from suffering. May I be healed. May I be at peace."[78]

This particular chant is part of a much longer meditation that repeats the basic intention of directing kindness toward the self and others. Working with a compassion practice opens us to the possibility of moving away from harboring judgments that keep us separate from others. We begin to see that all beings suffer, that harsh words and actions are a defense against pain, and that as we let go of judgments and opinions we find a reservoir of kindness within ourselves. As we repeat the meditation, we extend kindness outward in wider circles, until we embrace the whole world and feel our mutual connection as we repeat the phrase, "May all beings be free from suffering."[79]

When I first began using Levine's work, I was working with a man who was very angry with his brother. As a child he had felt betrayed by him in a profound way. He was truly tormented. As we worked together, he began to let in the possibility that all was not exactly as he had imagined; he, too, had played a part in the injury, and there was much more surrounding the painful events than he had realized. When he began to work with Levine's prayer and meditation, repeating the phrases of loving-kindness, he cried and cried as release washed over him. His own suffering seemed to merge with that of his brother's and with all who suffer. His anger receded like the tide and he felt calmer and quiet. It was a great lesson for me in understanding the power of forgiveness in easing human suffering, a pearl of wisdom.

In the forgiveness meditation, Levine invites you "to let yourself be loved. See your forgiveness forever awaiting your return to your heart." The gentle persistence and repetition of this meditation seems to work its way into consciousness by challenging long-held assumptions about who we are and what is possible. I am very grateful for Stephen and Ondrea Levine's heartfelt contribution to our understanding of grief, loss, loving-kindness, and forgiveness.

In my twenties, a friend gave me a very special book, *A Track to the Water's Edge*, by Olive Schreiner.[80] Born in South Africa at the time of the Boer Wars, Shreiner became a feminist who was sensitive to the powerful feelings and forces in her surroundings. In her book, she describes a series of dreams. One, in particular, "In a Ruined Chapel," has always stayed with me.[81] The story begins with a conversation between God and an angel. The angel has been to earth trying to help a man who says he cannot forgive someone who has wronged him. Having tried everything else, God gives the angel the power to return to earth and "unclothe a human soul, to take from it all those outward attributes of form, and color, and age, and sex, whereby one man is known from among his fellows and is marked off from the rest; and the soul lay before them, bare as a man turning his eye inward beholds himself."[82]

As the angel unclothes the soul of the other, the man realizes that he beholds no other than himself. The "other" is not separate but is the shadow side of himself, the part he feared and could not acknowledge or love. With this realization, he forgives him. He says, "How beautiful my brother is,"[83] and with this, he feels at peace.

Schreiner's story of seeing our mirror image in another person has stayed with me all these years; and when a client speaks of alienation from a family member or friend, her beautiful words return to me. So often, what we cannot forgive in the other is what we cannot accept in ourselves. Sometimes we are fortunate to find writing that touches us deeply, stories that give us a depth of understanding that stays with us throughout life. Olive Schreiner's stories have served me in this way.

In my own life, the search for a compassionate spiritual practice has old roots. Many years ago, when I was at the Santa Barbara swap meet, I saw a small, porcelain statue of a Chinese woman holding a flower. As I came closer, I was drawn to her beauty and her countenance. Her eyes had a downward gaze. I learned that this was a statue of Quan Yin, the Chinese Goddess of Compassion. I bought her for only $5.00. This began my love affair with the goddess. Representations of her compassionate qualities are found in many religious traditions. In China she is called by many names. She is the archetypal, loving Mother who hears the cries of the world.

Over the years, Quan Yin has sat in my office in my line of vision so that I can see her easily. Something in her gentle grace reminds me that compassion melts our fears. She has an infinite capacity to accept all that comes to her. She looks upon our self-perceived shortcomings and pours balm on them. As a therapist, you, too, may draw inspiration from this gentle goddess. She brings acceptance and compassion to all that troubles us. Having her image in my presence as well as my client's, feels essential to what I do.

Quan Yin and the hare have a very old association mythologically that dates back to the fourth century B.C. The hare is often pictured as inhabiting the moon where it is compounding the elixir of life. It is fascinating to me that my attraction to Quan Yin also led me to the hare and the moon. The moon is considered a symbol of the deep unconscious. The full moon is bright and shining like a pearl that illuminates the darkness. How intuitive we humans really are! Our myths and ancient stories confirm the power of our collective awareness.

Each of us comes to our work with insecurities and doubts. I say, use them all. Accept the many ways that you express who you are. Do not avoid or deny what is difficult in you. Instead, embrace it with respect and kindness, because that is your humanity and your calling.

In the Beginning Is the Ending

"What we call the beginning is often the end and to make an end is to make a beginning. The end is where we start from."
— T. S. Eliot [84]

The fact that all our beginnings will become endings is a difficult realization to hold. Most people are front-loaders — that is, we make a great deal of beginnings such as weddings, births, graduations, and new jobs. It is much harder to bring the same awareness to the endings or closings of these events. Retirement, illness, decline, divorce, and death — endings that we might not choose are inevitable. As clinicians, how do we stay awake to the reality of these profound changes and their certainty for both ourselves and our clients?

In graduate school, much emphasis is placed on making the initial connection with the client; but much less time and attention is spent on how to attend to closure. So now, as I come to the end of this book — a seven-year journey in my life — I want to take some time to address leavings and departures and how to stay present to the reality that in the beginning, the seeds of the ending have already been sown. are often more difficult than arrivals, although they are, of course, inextricable. Something, someone, or someplace must be left behind so that we can take the next step and allow new life to enter. The breath, like the heartbeat, takes us into another moment and another moment, until the energy of life passes away. Comings and goings are lessons of the moon. She is always waxing and waning in her cycle. Some say she is fickle, but I think not. She is changeable — and even that can be predicted in her cycles. She has lessons to teach us in this regard.

How do we handle the leavings and departures in psychotherapy? When is it time for a client to leave, and how do we know and prepare? Part of the shadow of psychotherapy is payment, and as psychotherapists our dependence upon that. We have a monetary and emotional stake in having clients come and stay. Our meetings become part of our schedule and part of our life. "It's Tuesday at 10:00," I say to myself. I know that I will see Susan. I look forward to her arrival. It is a rhythm, a kind of drum beat to which I respond. The shadow side of this rhythm is that as therapists, we can fall into a routine. We might even unconsciously collude with the client to avoid the inevitable departure and loss. After all, we enjoy seeing them, and our sessions have a certain momentum. As a result, we may fall into an unconscious attitude to avoid the ending of the relationship. All we can do is remind ourselves of the transience of the relationship and stay in tune with the work and how it is going.

I always ask a new client if they have had previous counseling and, if so, how that ended? Sometimes they say that they had trouble leaving their previous therapist. In some cases they stayed more than a year past their initial decision to end. Some describe the therapist's persuasiveness and suggestion that they were not ready to leave, as well as their own guilt and ambivalence. I feel it is best to honor the client's instincts in this regard. It is better to allow a client to leave gracefully when they choose to do so whether or not I agree. If I am concerned I may say so but I will not try to keep them. This supports their intuitive sense of what is best for them. I may not always agree and I will tell them so but I will also let them know that I support their decision. I remind them that they are welcome to return, if need be. There are times that clients leave without warning or discussion. This is generally difficult for me as I am left with unanswered questions. They miss an appointment or two and/or do not call. I reach out to them but often I am left with simply not knowing what happened. Did I screw up? Did I fail to notice something important or did it have nothing to do with me? Who knows? I surrender.

When therapist and client decide together that treatment is completed, both have to adjust to the inevitable change. When good work has been done, the client feels stronger and ready to depart. The therapist, like a good parent, needs to bring the work to closure and allow the client to leave gracefully and with our blessing. In truth, we will miss some clients more than others. For myself, endings are always poignant. Both the client and I have invested in the work and now the time for completion has arrived. You could say that we have an intuition, a sense, that it is time for us to change.

A few years ago, my husband built some birdhouses, one of them on a tree outside our window. Swifts took a liking to it. Every spring, the swifts return. For weeks there is great activity as the parents complete the nest inside the birdhouse. The babies are born and the cheeping begins and goes on for quite awhile. Meanwhile, the babies are growing. Then comes the day when a little head emerges in the round window of the box, and the baby bird looks out. The baby's head fills the hole. He does not hide when I pass but keeps looking out, seemingly assessing the world before him. We talk. Then one day I walk by and the little bird is gone. Occasionally, I have been there to see them take off. It is thrilling.

For myself, knowing when to bring therapy to closure is tied to a patient's movement in the sand tray. I have come to trust the process implicitly to give me a clear sense of when a client's work is completed or when a particular cycle is coming to a close. Most often, I observe the client's new interests arising or important shifts in emphasis. The client may display a feeling of optimism and a sense of capacity or willingness to be on her own. She may have an intention or new purpose, perhaps a spiritual impulse or pursuit. All these things signal a readiness to leave the safe haven of the therapeutic relationship. My tendency, too, is to trust the client. If she is sensing a readiness in herself and articulates that, I suggest moving from weekly to bi-weekly or monthly sessions for a limited time and easing into the departure. This allows time to reflect on the work we have done and the relationship between us. This gradual process works well, I believe, for both of us. Our time together is a spiraled process moving forward and backward, in and out. The client returns to important times and evocative experiences while simultaneously moving forward into the unknown.

There are also occasions when I have felt that therapy needed to come to a close and the client has felt otherwise. Sometimes, a dependency has grown up and the client wants to stay indefinitely. These are difficult situations that need to be worked through. All therapists have clients who return at different times when new stressors occur. This is a testimony to the strength of their bond and the feeling of safety that is available when needed.

All of this is to say that it is good to take the long view from the beginning, because there is a time when both client and therapist need to let go. Sometimes the ending of treatment is out of the therapist's hands and even the client's.

In the Beginning Is the Ending

There may be changes in your life as a therapist that involve sickness, yours or that of someone in your family, and possibly even a need to move to another area. (This occurred for me several times over the course of my professional life). Because of insurance, managed care, limited resources, and even court orders, there are times when the question of ending is influenced by a third party. Then the best you can do, of course, is talk about it. As soon as possible, introduce the fact that your time together will be limited. Then decide together how best to use the time that you have. I like to review a client's initial intention and see how they are feeling about it as we go along. Where and how do they see themselves in the process? These conversations are helpful in making adjustments, when necessary.

Leaving treatment can be difficult and highly charged. Endings are evocative of all previous leave-takings, some of which may have been traumatic. Psychotherapy is truly a journey. We do not know where it will take us nor do we know when it will come to an end. At best, the therapist needs to be sensitive to the inevitable shift in energy so that she or he can give the ending the attention it deserves.

The relationship between client and therapist is time-limited, even though we may meet regularly for several years. One could say that it has the illusion of permanence. Being a therapist means that everyone with whom we work will leave us; and at the same time, we remain indelibly connected. Each departure becomes a pearl in the chain of all those with whom we have worked and shared deeply.

The interplay of people, fortune, and experience of every kind, arriving and departing moment by moment, is the stuff of life. Thus, honor the ending as well as the beginning as each turns swiftly and inexorably into the next. The path of therapist and client is to walk together for a time, and then to separate when a new cycle calls. The client leaves in readiness for what is unfolding in his or her life. Meanwhile, the therapist has an "opening" for a new client as she weaves the spiral once again.

Resist Contrivance

Resist contrivance and certainty. Hold fast to what is of the body and soul and to what is not fully of this world. Make of each relationship a pilgrimage, a seeking.

My sense of therapy today is that it is an art that is being oppressed, or pressed down, less intimate, and practiced from a distance. At the same time, it has become increasingly mainstream. Just as in the practice of medicine, there is pressure to make psychotherapy more available through Skype or phone for people who are too busy for office visits or whose lives keep them in motion, traveling. I recognize that in physical medicine, Skype can be a great gift to those who do not live near services. My concern is that psychotherapy, in particular, will become disembodied and less personal. Are we willing to give up the immediacy of face-to-face encounter and replace it with Text-a-Therapist? Probably!

Recently, a client whom I have seen (in person, of course) for over two years told me that her insurance company had called her several times to ask if she would prefer to use Skype for her visits. In spite of her saying "no," they called her again. I was furious. I ranted. I am concerned that corporate health care, with its norms, requirements and monetary motive, is shaping the practice of psychotherapy.

There is always a pull from the collective toward conformity. Currently, this manifests in our profession through the monetizing of learning and training. Post-licensure is highly regulated, so that even after becoming licensed and working for many years to accomplish this goal, more training is required in the form of continuing education units or CEUs.

Therapy is increasingly promoted through workshops and trainings that promise to provide you with expertise, certification, and legitimacy. All kinds of "trainings" have been organized for your benefit. Every day I find that a new glossy brochure comes to me through the mail. For just $199.00 and 16 hours of my time, I can learn about some aspect of psychological treatment and satisfy the powers that be that I am not falling down on my job. I am amazed that almost every aspect of psychotherapy — such as anxiety disorders, eating disorders, trauma, or aging — is now a potential certification.

I have to ask, *who is really benefiting from this model of excellence?* After spending sufficient time and money, you can be certified post-licensure as an expert in some modality or population. The promise or implication is that when you use the new techniques you have learned, you will be able to practice with confidence and certainty. This is the shadow of "trainings." Promoting expertise *in this way* is an illusion promulgated for profit that reflects an overly masculine and hierarchical paradigm. Supplicants, both licensed and not, listen for many hours in a hall or watch on a screen. Usually, a large amount of information is supplied that cannot be digested in this form. At best, it may suggest new things to consider later, on your own, while leaving no room for mystery, unknowing, or uncertainty. In a patriarchy, certainty and assuredness are highly valued. They are things that you can bank on!

The proliferation of certifications feels like the old carrot-in-front-of-the-nose trick. Complete these requirements, accomplish these objectives and you, too, will be able to... (fill in the blank). Women, in particular, are susceptible to this paradigm of working harder and harder in order to prove themselves, indefinitely. We often feel that we are never quite enough and that the destination is always just a little further ahead. Many certifications are expensive and lengthy. Almost always, eventually, they take the form of institutes with levels of expertise or accomplishment, so that one becomes invested in going further and further, always chasing after the pinnacle of success and respectability.

I take exception to this kind of program because it discourages clinicians from learning through their own experience and inquiring on their own. We have been endowed with the gifts of imagination and creativity, if we trust ourselves to use them and follow the breadcrumbs wherever they may lead.

Rilke said it best in his advice to a young poet:

> I would like to beg you dear Sir to have patience with everything unresolved in your heart and to try to love *the questions themselves* as if they were locked rooms or books written in a foreign language. Don't search for answers that could not be given to you now because you would not be able to live them. And the point is to live everything. Live the questions now. Perhaps then, some day far into the future, you will gradually without even noticing it, live your way into the answer.[85]

I have honored Rilke's words for many years. Today, in reading them once again, this sentence stands out to me: "And the point is to live everything." Yes, live it all. Live bravely and exclude nothing. Allow the brave and curious hare to lead you. Trust your intuition.

In my personal history, I had a very painful experience in regard to the power of the establishment. I was a new and enthusiastic therapist, recently licensed. I had incorporated the sand tray into my work and used it often. I was excited about how effective it was. One evening I was seeing a couple. I had an intuition that using the tray would be a valuable experience for them. I suggested that they make a tray *together*. I was deliberately vague as to what or how, giving them a wide berth. I said that they could converse about it in any way they chose. The husband immediately took his finger and made a line down the center of the tray, suggesting that he take one side and that she take the other. With this simple gesture, I felt that he revealed much about the relationship dynamic, which could have taken much longer to understand through traditional verbal therapy. I knew instinctively and intuitively that using the tray with couples was a very valuable tool.

I continued working with couples and wrote an article "Sandplay with Couples" for *The Therapist*, a magazine published by the California Association of Marriage and Family Therapists.[86] A short time later, I received a letter from the Sandplay Therapists of America who were furious that I had branched out in this unsanctioned manner. How could I presume to do this? Their letter appeared in the front of the magazine in the "Opinion" section. I was quite shocked and devastated. I still believed in my work, but I was shaken and angry. Some time later they sent me a formal letter of apology, which I thought was to prevent me from suing them. I was too stunned and angry to respond.

I carried this wounding for quite some time and did not publish again for several years. I kept a low profile. I bring this up now because as a newly licensed therapist, you may also have new ideas and meet resistance from the powers that be. I hope that in these circumstances, you will find your voice and your confidence. I regret my silence many years ago and hope that in a small way I can make amends here by sharing this story with you.

Resist Contrivance

For over thirty years, I gave trainings for therapists who wanted to learn about sand tray work. When I taught it, I spoke to small groups. I aspired to openness in my presentation and I offered hands-on work. I encouraged students to think for themselves and to inquire deeply into their own process. When observing sand trays, I pay close attention to the client as well as to the development of the tray. I am very familiar with all of the figures in my collection and their symbolic meanings, but I resist excessive theorizing about what I am seeing in the tray. Of course, I have thoughts and impressions as well as feelings, sensations and intuitions concerning the configuration of things placed in the tray but I hold them in suspension, awaiting more information to come. I believe that the deepest healing occurs for the client in the making of the tray, and only they can know what it truly means to them. Interpretation is guesswork at best and, at times, a distraction.

Some years ago the Sandplay Therapists of America obtained a copyright for "sandplay." Because I am not a member of this organization, I refer to the work I have done for thirty years as *sand tray* therapy.

So for those of you who are called to become practitioners of the art of therapy, I say: *resist contrivance and certainty*. In this time when the Internet opens so many possibilities for human connection through texting, email, Skype, etc., the importance of sitting face-to-face, body-to-body with another person becomes all the more meaningful. Our words are not cut off and abbreviated. The phone does not anticipate our meaning and give us words before we can even complete them. We do not communicate through Emojis. We do what human beings have always done; we talk and listen, making eye contact, together.

I read recently that there are more people taking a pilgrimage of some kind today than ever before. There are more people walking the planet seeking a spiritual solution to what ails them. This is a powerful fact. The human heart has needs that cannot be resolved in an impersonal way. We humans need an intimate connection. How we find meaning and salvation is a matter of soul, heart, tears, and compassion. Where and how we put our feet down on this earth matters. And so, I say again: resist contrivance and certainty. Hold fast to what is of the body and soul, and make each relationship a pilgrimage, a seeking.

Last Thoughts

In recent months I have been captivated or captured by a Buddhist koan: "The moon sets at midnight. I walk alone through the town." A koan embeds itself in your mind/heart/body. I turn it over like a flapjack, this way, and that way. What does it mean? Does it mean anything? And yet it returns like a puzzle without a solution, like a friend who walks along beside me through the mystery.

The moon has accompanied me every day of my life like a silent partner. I have painted her many times. I love that she is mercurial, ever changing and yet always present. When I awaken during the night, I often go outside to see her, to say hello. She is a companion to my awakenings, whether in her slimmest crescent form or most effulgent wholeness. In China they often picture Quan Yin, the Goddess of Compassion with a hare in the moon. Here they are then, this wonderful triumvirate: the Moon, the Hare, and the Pearl of wisdom, together as an archetypal presence.

What is it like for me to come to the end of this book? It is both a huge relief and a great sadness. I have carried "the book" with me all over the world, and it has carried me. I have safeguarded my computer as if it were my lifeblood. The book has brought me great comfort and great challenge. It has been my companion at 3 a.m., 6 a.m., midnight, and every time in between. The computer has been there with its invitation to write and write more, to express ideas and to revel in the beauty of words and language. I hope that I have been able to express the profound love and respect I have for psychotherapy and those who practice it. I feel deep gratitude for the opportunities I have had to work in this heartfelt and creative way.

To my fellow therapists, I want to say that the art of therapy is *your* art, and there can be no other. You know better than anyone how healing lives in you and how your own suffering is the stuff of transformation that makes you who you are. I feel much gratitude for the opportunity to have shared my love of this work with you.

Psychotherapy, as I know it, is a healing art, an expressive and intuitive practice that is always evolving. Becoming a psychotherapist requires a deep commitment. Not only is the path long, arduous, and expensive, but it also asks everything of you. It asks you to offer up your being in service to another person. It asks you to attend, to hold, and to heal yourself as well as your client. The path is a calling; and each of us falls in love with the work in her own way.

May the work we do benefit all beings.

Much love and well-wishing to you,

Jenaii

Endnotes

Epigraph

Rumi, Jalul-uddin. *Teachings of Rumi: The Masnavi.* Translated and abridged by E. H. Whinfield. New York: Dutton, 1975, p. 191.

Sexson, Linda. *Ordinarily Sacred.* Charlottesville and London: University of Virginia Press, 1992, p. 1.

Jung, C. G. "Psychological Types," in *The Collected Works of C. G Jung*, Vol. 6. Revision by R. F. C. Hull of the translation by H. G. Baynes. Bollingen Series. Princeton, NJ: Princeton University Press, 1971 (originally 1953), p. 453.

Acknowledgments

1. Hesse, Hermann. *Magister Ludi: The Glass Bead Game.* New York: Bantam Books, 1970. Originally published as *Das Glasperlenspiel* by Richard and Clara Winston, Germany, 1943.

Preface

2. Singer, June. *Seeing Through the Visible World: Jung, Gnosis and Chaos.* New York: Harper One, 1991, p. 16.

3. Wolkstein, D., and Kramer, S. N. *Inanna: Queen of Heaven and Earth.* New York: Harper & Row, 1983, p. 155.

4. Ibid.

Introduction

5. *Random House Dictionary of the English Language*, Unabridged Edition, Jess Stein, Ed. New York: Random House, 1973.

6. Guru Maharaj Ji, 1972.

7. Daumal, R., *Mt. Analogue.* New York: Overlook Press, 2004. Originally published by Vincent Stuart Ltd., London, 1959.

8. Ibid., p. 43.

9. Ibid.

Part I: Invoking Your Intuition

Chain of Pearls

10. Markell, Jane. *Sand, Water and Silence: The Embodiment of Spirit*. London and Philadelphia: Jessica Kingsley Publishers, 2002, p. 56.

11. Von Franz, Marie-Louise. *Alchemy*. Toronto: Inner City Books, 1980.

12. Forge, Andrew. *Soutine*. London: Spring Books/Paul Hamlyn Ltd., 1965.

13. Ibid., p. 8.

14. Ibid., p. 11.

Handmaidens of Intuition

15. Canova, Antonio. Statue, "The Three Graces," 1814-1817. Wikipedia.

16. Connelly, Diane. *Traditional Acupuncture: The Law of the Five Elements*. Columbia, MD: Center for Traditional Acupuncture, 1979, p. 67.

17. Ibid.

Synchronicity — The Coincidence of Time and Space

18. *I Ching or the Book of Changes*. German translation by Richard Wilhelm, rendered into English by Cary F. Baynes. New York and London: Bollingen Series XIX, 1950; 3rd edition, 1967.

19. C. G. Jung, Foreword to the *I Ching, or Book of Changes*, translated by Richard Wilhelm. Princeton, NJ: Princeton University Press, 1950 (Bollingen Foundation, Inc., NY), p. xxiii.

20. *Random House Dictionary of the English Language*, Unabridged Edition, Jess Stein, Ed. New York: Random House, 1973.

21. Jung, C. G. "Synchronicity: An Acausal Connecting Principle," in *The Structure and Dynamics of the Psyche* (CW 8), pp. 506 ff.

22. Nichols, S. *Jung and Tarot: An Archetypal Journey*. NY: Samuel Weiser Publishers, 1980, p. 67.

23. Ibid.

Filings to the Magnet

24. Nelson, G. M. *Here All Dwell Free: Stories to Heal the Wounded Feminine*. New York: Doubleday, 1991, pp. 11-15.

Endnotes

Intuition: The Self and the Four Functions

25. Hollis, J. *Finding Meaning in the Second Half of Life*. New York: Gotham Books, 2005, pp. 4-5.

26. Jung, C. G. *Psychological Types*. In R. F. C. Hull (Revision of H. G. Baynes, Trans.), *The Collected Works of C. G. Jung*, Vol. 6. Princeton, New Jersey: Princeton University Press, 1974 (original work 1953), pp. 454-455.

27. Ibid.

28. Ibid., p. 455.

29. Ibid.

Following the Breadcrumbs

30. Grimm, Jacob and Wilhelm. *Grimm's Complete Fairy Tales*. UK: A. & C. Black, 1933, p. 44.

31. Ibid.

32. Baum, L. Frank. *The Wonderful Wizard of Oz*. Originally published 1900, reprinted by SDE Classics, 2019.

PART II: TRICKS OF THE TRADE
Backward Turning

33. Hirschfield, J. *Entering the Mind of Poetry*. New York: Harper Perennial, 1997, p. 26.

34. Ibid., p. 26.

35. Ibid.

36. Ibid.

The Art of Attention

37. Wikipedia, "Hermes."

Discerning Pattern

38. Phillips, Erma, *The Guiding Light* (soap opera, 1937-2009). New York: NBC, ABC, and CBS TV networks.

39. Winsor, R., and Nixon, A. *Search for Tomorrow* (soap opera, 1951-1976). New York: NBC TV network.

40. Freud, Sigmund. *Repetition Compulsion*. In *Errinnern, Wiederhofen, und Durchurbelten*, 1917.

41. Shapiro, Francine. *Eye Movement Desensitization and Reprocessing: Basic Principles, Protocols, and Procedures*. New York: Guildford Press, 2001.

42. Jung, C. G. "Psychological Types," in *The Collected Works of C. G Jung*, Vol 6. Revision by R. F. C. Hull of the translation by H. G. Baynes. Bollingen Series. Princeton, NJ: Princeton University Press, 1971 (originally 1953), p. 366.

Symptom as Messenger

43. Hillman, James. *Revisioning Psychology*. New York: Harper Perennial, 1976, p. 75.

44. *Diagnostic and Statistical Manual of Mental Disorders*, Fifth Edition. American Psychiatric Association.

45. *Random House Dictionary of the English Language*, Unabridged Edition, Jess Stein, Ed. New York: Random House, 1973.

Creativity and Addiction

46. Leonard, Linda. *Witness to the Fire: Creativity and the Veil of Addiction*. Boston and London: Shambhala, 1990.

Sitting with Loss

47. Romanyshyn, Robert. Lecture, Pacifica Graduate Institute, "Psyche-Centered Therapy II," 1995.

48. Hillman, James. *Revisioning Psychology*. New York: Harper Perennial, 1976, p. 75.

49. Mogenson, Greg. *Greeting the Angels: An Imaginal View of the Mourning Process*. Amityville, NY: Baywood Publishing Co., 1992, p. xii.

50. Ibid., p. 120.

Curiouser and Curiouser

51. Carroll, Lewis. *Alice's Adventures in Wonderland*. Boston, MA and Bath, England: Barefoot Books, 1993, pp. 2-3.

The Gift of Sand and Water

52. Kalff, Dora. *Sandplay: A Psychotherapeutic Approach to the Psyche*. Boston, MA: Sigo Press, 1980, p. 38.

53. Ibid., p. 37.

54. Ibid.

55. Jung, C. G. *Memories, Dreams and Reflections*. Recorded and edited by Aniella Jaffe. New York: Vintage Books, a division of Random House, 1961, pp. 174-175.

56. Kalff, D. *Sandplay: A Psychotherapeutic Approach to Psyche.*

Part III: Psychotherapist as Trickster — or, Crazy Like a Hare
The Sacrifice of the Hare, and the Healing Dream

57. Layard, John. *The Lady of the Hare: A Study in the Healing Power of Dreams*. Boston, MA and Shaftsbury, England: Shambhala, 1988, p. 49.

58. Ibid.

59. Ibid., p. 46.

60. Ibid., p. 222.

61. Ibid., p. 46.

62. Ibid., p. 42.

63. Knight, Peter. *Stolen Images: Pagan Symbolism and Christianity*. Wiltshire, UK: Stone Seeker Publishing, 2015, pp. 100-102.

LOL

64. *I Love Lucy*, Desilu Productions. American television sitcom starring Lucille Ball, originally running on CBS (1951-1957).

Meeting the Gypsy

65. Dylan, Bob. "Went to See the Gypsy." Recorded in 1970.

Skillful Means

66. Estes, Clarissa P. *Women Who Run with the Wolves*. New York: Ballantine Books, 1992, p. 39.

67. Ibid., p. 44.

Part IV: On the Practice of Suffering and Joy
Theater and Therapy

68. *Random House Dictionary of the English Language*, Unabridged Edition, Jess Stein, Ed. New York: Random House, 1973.

69. Stanislavski, Constantin. *Creating a Role*. New York: Theater Arts Books, 1961, p. 9.

70. Kopp, Sheldon. *This Side of Tragedy: Psychotherapy as Theater*. Palo Alto, CA: Science and Behavior Books, 1977.

71. Ibid., p. 4.

72. Kalff, Dora. *Sandplay: A Psychotherapeutic Approach to Psyche*. Boston: Sigo Press, 1980. As quoted by Harold Stone in the prologue to her book.

73. Ibid.

Psychotherapy as Confession

74. Hesse, Hermann. *Magister Ludi: The Glass Bead Game*. New York: Bantam Books, 1970. Translated from the German *Das Glasperlenspiel* by Richard and Clara Winston, originally printed in 1943.

75. Ibid., p. 454.

76. Ibid., p. 456.

Kindness Toward the Self

77. Levine, Stephen. *Healing into Life and Death*. New York: Anchor Press/Doubleday, 1989, pp. 98-101.

78. Ibid., p. 23.

79. Ibid., p. 26.

80. Schreiner, Olive. *A Track to the Water's Edge: The Olive Schreiner Reader*, Howard Thurman, Ed. New York: Harper and Row, 1973.

81. Ibid.

82. Ibid.

83. Ibid.

In the Beginning Is the Ending

84. Elliot, T. S. "Little Gidding."

Resist Contrivance

85. Rilke, Rainer Maria. *Letters to a Young Poet*. New York: W. W. Norton & Co., 1993.

86. Gold, J. "Sandplay with Couples," *The California Therapist*. San Diego, CA: Jan-Feb. 1993, pp. 53-57.

About the Author

 Jenaii Gold, Ph.D., MFT, has been a Marriage and Family Therapist since 1987. She received her doctorate from Pacifica Graduate Institute in Carpinteria, CA. In addition to being in private practice, she has supervised and mentored students for over thirty years. The experience of mentoring was her initial impulse for writing *The Moon, the Hare, and the Pearl*.

Gold writes from the perspective of the Crone, the wise old woman who has arrived at the third stage of her life. No longer the Maiden or ingénue, no longer the Mother, she sits with the Grandmothers of this world who oversee the new and becoming.

She has conducted workshops and trainings on sand tray therapy, creativity, and the Feminine. She is currently in private practice in Santa Barbara, California, where she lives with her husband, Eric, and her cat, Moo Cow Kitty.

Should you wish to contact her, she can be reached by:

Email: *jenaiigold1@gmail.com*

Phone: (805) 845-6609

Or on her website: *www.jenaiigold.com*

www.ingramcontent.com/pod-product-compliance
Lightning Source LLC
Chambersburg PA
CBHW021105080526
44587CB00010B/383